Ancient Ancestors

of the Southwest

Photography by Lewis Kemper

Text by Gregory Schaaf

GRAPHIC ARTS CENTER PUBLISHING®

Table of Contents

Acknowledgments 7
Introduction 9
Roots of the Ancient Southwest 13
Beginnings 19
Pueblo Life 29
Ancient Peoples of Arizona 39
Ancient Peoples of Utah 49
Ancient Peoples of New Mexico 57
Ancient Peoples of Colorado 69
Epilogue 75
Clans & Sites 76
Index 78
Site Map 81 (Inside Back Cover)

The interpretations in this book have been drawn
from traditional oral histories, from elders, the writings
of professional scholars, the field work of archaeologists,
original historic documents, and personal observations.

International Standard Book Number 1-55868-255-4
Library of Congress Number 96-75274
Photographs © MCMXCVI by Lewis Kemper
Text © MCMXCVI by Gregory Schaaf
The images at the openings of each chapter are from
the collection of Edge of the Cedars State Park, Utah.
No part of this book may be copied by any means
without written permission from the publisher.
President • Charles M. Hopkins
Editor-in-Chief • Douglas A. Pfeiffer
Managing Editor • Jean Andrews
Photo Editor • Diana S. Eilers
Project Editor • Suzan Hall
Designer • Robert Reynolds
Production Manager • Richard L. Owsiany
Book Manufacturing • Lincoln & Allen Co.
Printed and bound in the United States of America

Front Cover Photo: *An unnamed cliff dwelling.* Half Title Page: *A kiva interior
(Kakora) at Pecos Pueblo, Pecos National Monument, New Mexico. It was occupied by
Pe-Kush Pecos, circa* A.D. *1300 to 1838.* Frontispiece: *White House Ruin in Canyon
de Chelly National Monument, Arizona. De Chelly was occupied by Basketmakers,
Hopi, and Tewa—ancestors of the Asa, Wild Mustard Clan—circa* A.D. *850 to 1390.*
Opposite Page: *Mano in aligned doorways, Aztec Ruins National Monument, New
Mexico. This area was occupied by San Juan River peoples circa* A.D. *1100 to 1300.*

To all our ancient ancestors
whose courage, determination and spirit
nourish the roots of our common heritage.

LEWIS KEMPER AND GREG SCHAAF

Acknowledgments

I would like to thank all of those employees of the National Park Service, the Forest Service, and the BLM who spend their lives to protect and to interpret these sites for us to enjoy, especially those who led me on tours. I would also like to thank James Cunkle and the folks at White Mountain Archaeological Center for their hospitality during adverse weather, to Ernest House for his tour of Ute Mountain Tribal Park, to Virginia Austin and her wranglers at Navajo National Monument, to Fred Hirschmann for directions, and to Todd Prince of Edge of the Cedars State Park.

A special thanks to my sister Ellen for introducing me to Greg Schaaf, and to her family for putting up with my visits to Sante Fe, to my parents and family for always supporting my choice to be a photographer, and to Michael Broome for accompanying me on the last trip to the ruins. I have a heartfelt thank you to my wife Heidi for keeping me company when she could, and for being patient with me when she could not.

LEWIS KEMPER

In acknowledging the many who helped make this book possible, first recognition belongs to the Indian elders who inspired the project with a simple request: "Find all the documents related to our history and culture." Most of those elders are not identified here by name, out of respect for their privacy. Thanks to our friends at Hopi, Zuni, Taos, Picuris, Sandia, Isleta, San Juan, Santa Clara, San Ildefonso, Nambe, Tesuque, Pojoaque, Jemez, Pecos, Acoma, Cochiti, Laguna, San Felipe, Santa Ana, Santo Domingo, Zia, Navajo, and Apache.

Support for our research efforts came from many institutions, including the universities of New Mexico, Arizona, Colorado, and Utah; School of American Research; Museum of Indian Arts and Cultures; Wheelright Museum; Heard Museum; Institute of American Indian Arts; National Museum of the American Indian; and the Smithsonian Institution, and more. Rare book dealers worked as historical detectives, especially Bob Craner and Bob Fein, and the staffs of Books Unlimited, Dumont Maps and Books, Books and More Books, Collected Works Bookshop, Old Santa Fe Trail Book Store, Margolis and Moss Books.

The directors of Southwest Learning Centers also deserve recognition. They are Seth Roffman, Radford Quamahongnewa, Dane Reese, Frances Harwood, John Kimmey, Gail Russell, James Berenholtz, Mazatl Galindo, and Fidel Moreno. Jeffrey Bronfman's vision and support inspires us all.

Our gratitude to Ellen Kemper and Ken Hughes, who introduced the author to the photographer and helped proofread, and others who offered editorial suggestions, including Luella Schaaf, Kim, David, and Tony Moore, Blanche Brody, Sondra Seymour, Wayne Lawrence, and Maggie Banner. The author's literary agent, Al Zuckerman of Writers House, is commended for his good faith.

Collections large and small, public, private, and tribal have aided greatly in our search for knowledge. We continue to benefit from efforts for cultural preservation. Our national and state parks, archeological preserves, and tribal lands are rich sources of information. Let us treat them with highest respect.

GREGORY SCHAAF

◄▲ *"Nachwach" or "Reunion" symbols show ceremonial handshakes used to identify clans after migrations. The petroglyphs lie near Puerco Ruins, Petrified Forest National Park, Arizona.*
◄ *"Nachwach" or "Reunion" symbols decorate a black-on-white mug at Edge of the Cedars State Park, Utah, Pueblo III.*

Introduction

I believe it is important for parents to teach their children about this land's original people, their environment and their traditional ways. When we know their stories, Kokopelli plays his magic flute, and thousands of ancient ruins, from Mesa Verde to Chaco Canyon, come to life. The teachings of the elders, passed down from generation to generation through clans, touch our lives with the wisdom of humanity.

Clan histories unlock the history of the Southwest. More than two hundred groups of extended families, or clans, survive. Their elders can still tell the traditional creation stories and recite sagas of long migrations comparable to the Odyssey, the journeys of the tribes of Israel, or the adventures of Marco Polo. These rich oral histories give us insights into the lives of the people who explored this beautiful land in the beginning—grandmothers and grandfathers, parents and children walking up and down the river valleys, over majestic mountains, spiraling inward, searching for the world's center.

Now, with the help of archeological evidence, scientific methods, and fast computers, we are beginning to authenticate their stories and put the fragments of history in chronological sequence. A clearer, more personal history of the ancient Southwest is coming into focus.

Southwest Learning Centers has been dedicated to the preservation of Southwest arts and cultures for the past twenty-four years. Our archives expand daily, and our activities touch people's lives—a growing school curriculum and special programs that range from reviving classic Pueblo textile techniques to helping elders through the winter.

My interest in the Southwest began in childhood, when my parents took us on summer trips and told family stories that added to our clan lore. Our grandparents taught us about eight different cultures in our family tree: Cherokee, Choctaw, French, English, Irish, Scottish, German, and Dutch. Travel and those family stories expanded our vision, gave us a sense of identity, and built our self-esteem.

My first friendships with Southwest Indians began in 1981, when I was a doctoral candidate in Indian history at the University of California, Santa Barbara. One day a man called and identified himself as a representative of high spiritual leaders of the Hopi, the "People of Peace." I thought one of my friends must be playing a trick on me.

◄ *Kokopelli Petroglyph, Rio Grande Valley, New Mexico. This Mesoamerican figure carried vegetable seeds in his backpack.*

The man reassured me, explaining that Hopi elders had read a series of articles I had written on Indian treaties and sovereign rights. I was invited to come to a gathering of Indian nations at Hopiland, about a hundred miles from the Grand Canyon. I accepted.

A young Aztec in an old pickup truck arrived shortly to take me on the adventure that changed my life. I will never forget the experience of reaching the top of the Hopi mesas, after riding all night. Thousand-year-old stone villages stood bathed in the orange mists of sunrise. Red cedar smoke curled from pueblo roof tops. Song birds warbled their morning chorus. Dogs barked as we bumped and rolled down dusty roads into the heart of the village.

Rain cloud symbols decorated the home where the pickup finally came to rest. A Hopi grandmother greeted us with loving hugs. We warmed our hands beside her potbelly stove as she brewed a pot of herbal tea and cooked a breakfast of blue corn dumplings and peaches.

Later, about two hundred people from across the country gathered outdoors, next to a cornfield, for the meeting. Grandma started the fire to "make it pure." Prayers were delivered. People all around the circle introduced themselves—Cree Indians from Canada, Aztecs from Mexico, Chumash from California, and Iroquois from New York. From the four directions, native people had gathered to talk about treaties, sovereignty, and their rights to determine their own futures. I felt shy when someone urged me into the center of the group to tell them all about treaties, especially the Treaty of Guadalupe Hidalgo.

Fortunately, I had brought over five thousand pages of treaties and historical documents. We talked deeper and deeper, then someone went to get the oldest elder in the village, Grandfather David Monongye. This one-hundred-year-old man, wearing glasses thick as the bottom of coke bottles, came walking down the trail, poking his cane confidently every step of the way. He eyed the stack of documents for a long time, then announced, "It was prophesied that one day a big stack of papers would be brought to us. The tradition foretold it would be at the bottom. That's where we'll find what's important!"

Curious and anxious, we dug to the bottom and found a copy of the official map of the 1848 Treaty of Guadalupe Hidalgo that ended the Mexican-American War. An Aztec man translated the Spanish text into English. A Hopi man translated English to Hopi. The notation on the map for Hopiland translated, "The Hopi have conserved their independence since 1680."

Grandfather David slapped his hand on his knee and proclaimed, "That's what we've been looking for! That proves both the United States and Mexico recognized our independence, our freedom, our sovereignty!"

The thrill of discovery filled the air. A young woman helped me bundle up the stack of papers and off we marched back to the center of the pueblo. I was led down into Grandfather David's kiva, an underground religious chamber symbolizing the "womb of Mother Earth." Several elderly men arrived, lit their black stone pipes and prayed for a long time. After their interpreter arrived, Grandfather David spoke at length in Hopi before introducing me. I spread out the big stack of papers on the dirt floor. We read key passages, searched deeper, and the elders spoke rapidly in Hopi. I had never seen a group of people get so excited about history.

During the following days and nights they shuttled me around to kivas and homes in various mesa villages. Everywhere the process was repeated. They questioned me for hours about background. They asked me to define the term, "liberty." I explained the origin from *Libertas*, the name of the woman who freed the slaves in ancient Greece.

Elders asked, "What did they mean when they said, '. . . the right to life, liberty and the pursuit of happiness'?" I explained that Jefferson and American Revolutionaries wanted to be free from British oppression, to be sovereign.

Then they asked, pointing to a key passage in the Treaty of Guadalupe Hidalgo, "What does it mean when the United States and Mexico promised to '. . . respect the liberty of the native people'?"

Before I could answer, another man asked, "Would it not be a violation of our liberty for our boys to be drafted? We are Hopis, People of Peace. War is against our religion!"

The dialogue continued late into the night, day after day. We tape-recorded our meetings at the elders' request. Finally, Grandfather David announced to me the elders' decision, "The United Nations is giving us five minutes to make a presentation. We have told you what is important. You're the writer. Write."

"Who, me?"

"Yes, you're the writer," Grandfather David asserted.

For twenty-four hours straight, I poured over the documents and tapes. I presented a first draft, as a freshman would to his professors. Much to my surprise, the elders scolded me.

"Why did you put this first? This sentence should be first. What does this word mean? We don't talk like that. This is the way we say it . . ." Hopi elders, I concluded, were the toughest editors on Earth.

Finally, after countless rewrites, I presented the latest draft. The elders sat hunched over, in total silence, puffing on their pipes. In unison, these wise old people uttered, "Huh! Uh-huh!" That was it, the Hopi version of winning the Pulitzer Prize. No slaps on the back, no exclamations of, "Good job!" Just a slight nod, and they set to work making prayer feathers. They blessed the paper, sprinkling cornmeal on the pages. Then their spokesmen rushed to the airport and flew off to the United Nations.

I thought my job was done, but it was only the beginning. I have served for fifteen years as historian to the Hopi elders, learning to follow the path of humility they value. Other papers written for them have included, "The Hopi Statement for the United Nations' Nuclear Disarmament Talks" and the "Hopi Prayer for Peace." The UN Secretary General read the prayer to the General Assembly in 1982.

Many of the elders I worked with originally—David, Claude, Earl, and others—have passed away. Before they passed to the next world, these elders asked me to collect every original Hopi document I could find. The first stack of five thousand pages has grown several stories high.

Before he passed away, Grandfather David said, "If you search your roots back far enough, your ancient ancestors originally were tribal people all over the world. Tribes were groups of clans, and clans were groups of families. Every clan was given a set of Original Divine instructions, like 'Thou shalt not kill.' These instructions are universal. If we live up to these responsibilities, this land and life will go on and on. This is the secret to peace."

The original Puebloan world view didn't see people as a race—red, black, white, or yellow—but rather as a "positive, productive people" or a "violent, destructive people." All have the capacity for both, but those who follow the path to destruction are said to have "two hearts."

A Tewa elder told me that even people who don't know their original clan can rediscover their true identity by considering this question, "If you believed in reincarnation, with which animal would you feel close kinship?" Some people imagine flying like an eagle, he said. Others connect with the bear. When he said, "Some men definitely are coyotes!" we laughed, but the message was clear. People around the world share common roots.

This book is about rediscovering what life was like for the Original People. Learning about their ways of life may inspire us to search for our own roots. Somewhere deep inside, we may discover what is unique and universal about each of us.

▲ *Wupatki National Monument, Arizona. This area was occupied by the Sinagua, Mogollon, and Kayenta peoples—ancestors of the Hopi—circa* A.D. *1075 to 1255.* ▶ *Algae and lichen were used for herbal dyes in natural fiber weaving; Canyonlands National Park, Utah.*

Roots of the Ancient Southwest

To the Original People of the Southwest, the Earth is sacred. Each mountain and valley, each river and spring is a holy place. Even the smallest mesa has a name, a spirit and a history. Elders explain that, when the ancient ancestors first emerged into this "World Complete," they made a covenant with the Great Spirit to reverence and protect their mother, Earth.

In this book, we follow trails worn smooth by footsteps over thousands of years, tracing clues to unveil the stories of countless generations, back to the dawn of time. Let us walk in harmony and beauty, with respect for this land, and for those who walked before us.

Scientific methodology and powerful computers are helping us build a chronological history of the Ancient Southwest. With modern dating techniques, we can now begin to link the information in oral histories with archaeological evidence to create a truer picture of the ancient ancestors' lives. The quantity of information is massive; the task is as daunting as matching the millions of pieces of pottery scattered over almost every acre of the Southwest.

We owe a debt to pioneer researchers like Elsie Clews Parsons, a remarkable folklorist and oral historian who devoted much of her life to following the legendary trail of the ancient Southwest. Working in the 1920s with an early Edison tape recorder, she encouraged tribal elders to record their memories, clan stories, and the histories handed down from earlier generations. The Smithsonian Institution's leading linguist, John Peabody Harrington, worked with her, and over a million pages of his field notes survive in the National Anthropological Archives. Others soon followed their lead, including such notables as Dr. Ruth Benedict, Franz Boas, W. W. Robbins, and B. Freire-Marreco.

Gradually, we are fitting the pieces of history together. Each story is part of an elaborate historical puzzle covering four states: Arizona, Utah, New Mexico, and Colorado. Initially, these pieces create monumental mosaics of stone palaces, astronomical towers, great houses and kivas, ball courts and multi-storied pueblos. Highly intelligent master masons, engineers, and priests designed these communities; their descendants now build most of the millionaires' estates in Santa Fe and Taos. Filling in the historical details

◄ A pine tree grows out of lava at Sunset Crater National Monument. This area of Arizona was occupied by the Sinagua ancestors of the Hopi during the time of the eruption of the volcano in A.D. 1064 and 1066.

simply deepens our respect for Native American artistic mastery and contributions to global culture.

Researching the past gives us new understanding of the less tangible part of Southwest culture: the spirituality that imbues every aspect of Native American life. At the beginning, as with all people, the family was the fundamental unit of organization. Next, people began to identify with the extended family, or clan. Among Native Americans in the Southwest, these clan ties followed matrilineal blood lines. Over time, clans banded together to form the larger units we call tribes or nations. The most illuminating information, which we are now gathering as oral history, has been handed down, generation by generation, through the clans.

Like a stone skipping across the waters of time, we can only touch on the historic highlights in the limited space of this book. Our touch points are thirty-three important Southwest sites. Our research rippled out from these landmarks, following the old trails connecting the Southwest through successive eras. Farther and farther we searched, back in time to the origins of existence.

Every clan, society, and tribe in the Southwest has stories of its origins. While they have many different names, cultures, and religions, we have not found a single clan that does not believe in a version of the common creation story. Living descendants affirm, and records of the Smithsonian Institution and other sources confirm, that this was true for every tribe—the Hopi, Zuni, Acoma, Cochiti, Laguna, San Felipe, Santo Domingo, Zia, Taos, Picuris, Sandia, Isleta, San Juan, Santa Clara, Nambe, San Ildefonso, Pojoaque, Tesuque, Jemez, Pecos, Navajo, Ute, Apache, Paiute, Papago, Shoshone, Yavapai, Walapai, and Pima, right down to the Havasupai in the bottom of the Grand Canyon. All were religious people with faith in the Creator and divine spirituality.

The Pueblo story of creation and evolution is told as a story of four worlds. This Fourth World, "World Complete," in which we now live, may not be the last. If people do not honor the covenant they made to protect the Earth and respect fellow creatures, Mother Earth may take matters into her own hands, bringing this world to a cataclysmic end, and beginning again. Today, some elders warn, we may already have one foot in the Fifth World.

Understanding the creation stories requires that we bend our minds away from the confining concept of linear time and think with the astrophysicists who explain that we are all made of the original stardust. If we think of matter as energy, then nothing is lost; it simply changes form. The ancient ancestors imbued everything with a powerful spirituality. That spirit is like energy; it always exists. The past is still present, though we may not be able to access it. To question the nature or sequence of the four worlds, or to question the details of the migration sagas that follow, is really irrelevant. It is the fundamental truths in the stories that matter.

First World: Tokpela, Endless Space

The Hopi call the First World *Tokpela*, "Endless Space." Tokpela was inhabited by *Sotukeu-nangwi*, the Supreme Being or Heavenly God, who envisioned existence. He was served by powerful heavenly bodies, among them *Taiowa*, the Sun Spirit, Spider Grandmother, and the little Twin War Gods. The spirit of the Earth, *Maasaw*, sometimes was addressed as the "Great Spirit." An elderly Blue Bird Clan Chief explained:

> Now will I begin from the very beginning of our traditional history of the Hopi. Somewhere the human life began. There are many stories of this beginning. The Hopi believe that Maasaw, the Great Spirit, was the leader and the Creator of our land. With him in the early beginning were the Spider Lady to keep the fire and her two nephews [Twin War Gods]. These were the four of the beginning.

Southwest Natives believed that all forms of life are endowed with soul or spirit and are part of the Great Spirit.

According to modern science, the sun helped create life on Earth by making it possible for the first single-celled organisms to create life-giving oxygen. Tewa Indians also believe the sun played an essential role in the development of life. One Tewa elder explained:

> Now, there was a Great Spirit watching over everything, and some people say he was Tawa, the sun. He saw how things were down under the earth. He didn't care for the way the creatures were living. He sent his representative, Gogyeng Sowuhti, Spider Old Woman, to talk to them. She said, "You creatures, the Sun Spirit who is above doesn't want you living like this. He is going to transform you into something better, and I will lead you to another world."

Second World: Tokpa, Destroyed by Fire

The powerful lesson of the Second World is in its name: *Tokpa*, "Destroyed by Fire." The Earth's creatures should have lived happily in this Second World, but they forgot their primary purpose—to carry out the Creator's plan.

Cataclysm—fires, floods, and famine—frequently mark history's transition points between eras or worlds. The Great Flood in the Bible is just one example.

Sun Clan leader Dan Katchongva recorded this account of creation in 1973, when he was one hundred years old:

> Somewhere down in the Underworld we were created by the Great Spirit, the Creator. We were created first one, then two, then three. We were created equal, of oneness, living in a spiritual way, where the life is everlasting. We were happy and at peace with our fellow men. All things were plentiful, provided by our Mother Earth upon which we were placed. We did not need to plant or work to get food. Illness and troubles were unknown. For many years we lived happily and increased to great numbers.

> When the Great Spirit created us, he also gave us instructions. We promised to live by his laws so that we would remain peaceful . . . by and by we broke the Creator's command. So he punished us by making us as we are now, with both soul and body. He said, "From now on you will have to go on your own. You will get sick, and the length of your life will be limited."

> He made our bodies of two principles, good and evil. The left side is good for it contains the heart. The right side is evil for it has no heart. The left side is awkward but wise. The right side is clever and strong, but it lacks wisdom. There would be a constant struggle between the two sides, and by our actions we would have to decide which was stronger, the evil or the good.

Tewa tradition from New Mexico echoes those teachings. Explaining why the Second World was destroyed, one Sun Clan leader said:

> The creatures didn't behave well. They didn't get along. They ate one another. There was chaos and dissension. So the Great Spirit sent Gogyeng Sowuhti [Spider Grandmother] down again after he transformed those beings without tails into a human like form. But they weren't yet true humans, because they were undisciplined. Gogyeng Sowuhti led them to another world up above, the Third World.

This transformation of "beings without tails into a human like form" is what scientists call the evolution. The great debate between scientists and religious fundamentalists, which climaxed in the "Monkey Trial," is considered humorous by many Indians.

One elder remarked, tongue in cheek, "I listened to both sides and concluded those anthropologists probably really did come from monkeys! They're from the Monkey Clan. We are Bear Clan, Deer Clan and many more. We were born from Mother Earth. What do they call it, the 'primal ooze'?"

He went on to explain that some clans believe they are related to their totem animal—like Bear Clan people who get up in the morning "like hungry bears. Everyone's heard stories of those wily Coyotes!"

Third World: Kuskurza, The Underworld

The Third World of the Hopi, Kuskurza, is under the surface of the Earth. It is both the place where the ancient ancestors lived after their Second World was destroyed and the place where everyone goes after death. It is not hell or a place of punishment. Hopis describe their final resting place as Wajima, a kiva-like place in the Underworld, inside Mother Earth. Wajima Lake is said not to be a real lake, but the "dancing hall of spirits."

Many Pueblo people recount how their ancestors once lived in the Underworld before they were born from Mother Earth. In that Underworld, or Third World, there was apparently some form of evil, or at least the people encountered some temptations.

One Sun Clan elder explained that they called it the "Underworld" because, ". . . there the living stream changed from good into corruption."

We lived in good ways for many years, but eventually evil proved to be stronger. Some of the people forgot or ignored the Great Spirit's laws. The life of the people became corrupted with social and sexual license. Soon the leaders and others with good hearts were worried that the life of the people was getting out of control. The Kikmongwi gathered the high priests. They smoked and prayed for guidance toward a way to solve the corruption.

Pueblo and other Native people have long traditions of respecting the power of prayer. Modern science is now confirming that value. The American Medical Association recently recognized that prayers and meditation can be healing. People around the world, from many faiths, have acclaimed prayer for saving their lives. Medical researchers now have proved that the power of positive thinking is real. Some family counselors also have found that praying together may help families heal their divisions. The opposite, negative behavior, can make people physically ill.

In the Native American community, someone who intentionally hurts others sometimes is referred to by the old term, sorcerer. Sorcerers were blamed for corrupting the Underworld; there were sorcerers who made people fall sick or quarrel with one another. The evil ones made life hard for everyone. *Gogyeng Sowuhti*, Spider Grandmother, told them, "Above us is the Fourth World. Up there life will be better for you."

According to elders' stories:

. . . they prayed in harmony, singing holy songs, to open a passageway into the next world. Some say a sacred tree grew, others a hollow reed, that pierced the sky. They climbed up, one by one, toward the Fourth World.

Fourth World: Tuwaqachi, World Complete

Ancient ancestors of Puebloan people, according to spiritual traditions, emerged into the Fourth World from *Sipapu*, the navel of Mother Earth.

Hopi and Zuni traditions describe their emergence from deep in the Grand Canyon. Other accounts place *Sipapu* variously from the bottom of the Grand Canyon to the Rocky Mountains.

The Keresan account says:

. . . emergence into the world was a great act of the Spirit for it came about with reverence and love for what was left behind in the spirit world . . . from the womb of the earth . . . the Spirit guided the ancient people . . . across this great continent southward, until they came to settle temporarily in the places of today's National Parks and National Monuments . . .

The Towa are said to have emerged at Wavinatita, a lagoon near Stone Lake in northern New Mexico, south of Dulce. They were still living there in A.D. 1.

Some say the Tewa place of emergence, *Sipofenae*, was under a lake in southern Colorado. Others place it in Great Sand Dunes National Monument near Alamosa, Colorado. The Tewa then moved into the Rio Grande Valley.

According to Tewa-Hopi elder Albert Yava:

. . . the story told to us by our elders is that the Tewas originated at a place called Sibopay. In some respects the story is similar to that of the Hopis. It says that the people came from down below. There weren't humans down there, only creatures of different kinds, and they emerged by climbing a tall spruce or pine. When they came out on the surface of the earth, that's when they became humans. The people who came out were Tewas, not mixed tribes as in the Hopi tradition. The sacred place where this happened is regarded as the navel of the earth. There's a lake over in Colorado, a briny lake, that's called Sibopay.

The identity of Tewa people is connected with their common origins at the place of emergence. First Mesa Tewas sing the story every winter:

Somewhere, somewhere,
Far away,
What were you at Sibopay when you were born?
That is what I am asking,
What am I myself going to be?

The long chant explains the nature of life, birth, childhood and how to act like a responsible adult until "the Great Spirit calls you."

The Great Migrations

When the ancient ancestors emerged into the Fourth World, the Great Spirit *Maasaw* not only exacted an agreement from them to preserve and protect the land, but also instructed them to go out in the Four Directions to explore and claim it for him. The great migration sagas are the stories of that exploration to the outer reaches of the Western Hemisphere—to the coasts, north to Alaska, and to the tip of South America—then their return, and each clan's search for its rightful "Center Place."

Zuni tradition includes a poetic description of their migrations in search of the center of the world, the "Middle Place," *Itiwana*. It explains how they reached out like the arms of a Water Strider, an insect with broad legs that allow it to float on the water:

He touched the corners of the east and north, but could not touch the corners of the west and south. He said, "You are very near. I will go and find the place where my arms will touch the horizon in all four directions." The bow priests went with him. Water Spider said, "I have to go back. Let us try Halona (ant place). My heart will be on an anthill." He stretched out his arms and legs and touched the horizon at the north, west, south and east. He was in the middle of the world. He said, "My people shall live here always. They will never be overthrown for their hearts will not be to one side of the world."

Searching for their center place, the Keresan people moved south to a place called White House. Through spiritual teachings of clan leaders, they learned how to live in harmony with the Earth. However, as history so often repeats itself, quarreling disrupted society. *Iyatiko*, Mother Earth, caused each quarreling faction to speak a different language. Different religious societies were created, and groups of clans eventually settled in their present pueblos: Acoma, Cochiti, Laguna, San Felipe, Santa Ana, Santo Domingo, and Zia.

Zia tradition explains that the quarrel at the White House developed between men and women, and the women ". . . boasted that they could do without men."

To test them, the men crossed a river to live alone. Some women "couldn't stand it" and stole across at night to have intercourse. Their offspring were born monsters who terrified all mankind. A virgin daughter of the tiyamunyi [head Zia spiritual leader], impregnated by the Sun, then gave birth to Masewi and Oyoyewi, the Twin War Gods, who journeyed about destroying the monsters and serving as protectors of the people ever since.

The origin of the Parrot Clan is a multi-generational saga of a great migration from the bottom of the Grand Canyon to the tip of South America and back again. The late Jacob Bahnimptewa, a respected member of the Parrot Clan, once stayed up all night to tell me the saga of his ancestors:

They walked southward through Mexico. Some liked the beautiful central valley and stayed to become the Aztecs. The main group kept walking and encountered the Mayans in Central America. High in the Andes, they visited the Incan Empire. Following the mountains and the coastline, they finally arrived at the farthest point in the South. A shrine was created there to claim this land for Maasaw, the Spirit of the Earth.

Their spiritual instructions fulfilled, the people turned around and headed northward.

While in the Amazon rainforest, the women began to miscarry. Babies were born dead. The people feared the entire clan might die out before returning to the Mother Village at Hopi. A medicine man, a healer from one of the Amazonian tribes, appeared and offered the women herbal medicines. Like a blessing, healthy babies were born. All were grateful. As they were departing northward, the Amazonian medicine man gave them gifts of parrot feathers. In honor of this healing, they renamed their babies to be *Kyashngyam*, meaning "Parrot Clan."

The Parrot Clan is most closely related to the *Katsinyam* or Kachina Clan. The term *Kachina* or *Katsina* can refer to spiritual beings, members of their religious societies, or images carved or painted.

The Tewa migration stories recount their arrival at Oga'akeneh, a big body of water. There they divided into many clans. The main group crossed water and arrived at Shonkyugeh, Slippery Point. Others branched away until they settled in their present Rio Grande pueblos: San Juan, Santa Clara, San Ildefonso, Nambe, Pojoaque, and Tesuque.

The stories are many and colorful; research is helping us match them with historic fact. By carefully searching clan stories related to specific ruins, groups of ancient ancestors can be traced to contemporary tribes. Today, their descendants live in pueblos, reservations, and communities throughout the Southwest.

For example, members of the Sun Clan from Chaco Canyon and Mesa Verde now live at every pueblo. The Bear Clan from Mesa Verde spread to Hopi, Acoma, Cochiti, Laguna, San Felipe, Santo Domingo, Zia, Taos, San Juan, Nambe, Jemez, and Zuni. Eighteen clans have stories of living at Mesa Verde, Betatakin, and Keet Seel. Twenty-eight clans claim to have lived at Homol'ovi, the important staging area south of Hopi. Seven clans are known to have lived at Montezuma's Castle. The Badger, Butterfly, and Wild Mustard Clans preserve stories of their ancestors living at Canyon de Chelly. Their descendants live at Hopi, First Mesa, Acoma, and Zuni. Twenty-one clans identify with Bandelier, mostly Keresan and Tewa speaking people.

What proof do we have that these clans lived at specific ancient sites? Their clan markings, pictographic symbols, appear nearby on rock walls. Pottery fragments with unique styles are found on the ground, "our title to the land," say some elders. Textile, basketry, and jewelry fragments, as well as architectural styles are among the clues.

Making direct links and dating specific sites sends the thrill of discovery coursing through a researcher's veins. Much work remains, but new methods for linking specific clans to ancient sites are opening up exciting new vistas.

▲ *The Lower Ruins at Tonto National Monument, Arizona. This area was occupied by the Salado people circa* A.D. *1100 to 1350.* ▶ *The mountains above the Salt River, for which the Salado people were named, are covered with saguaro cactus, cholla, and brittlebrush, Tonto National Monument, Arizona.*

Beginnings

The rich oral histories passed down from the ancient ancestors contain colorful stories to explain the creation of the earth, the origins of life and the development of culture. The nature of the first creatures, the importance of the stars, recurrent cataclysms, the cycles of destruction and rebirth—all are described. And all are surprisingly compatible with the story modern science has unfolded.

Scientists date the origin of the Earth at 4,600,000,000 B.C., a time named the Precambrian Era. Astrophysicists believe that every atom in our bodies and throughout the planet is from stardust. The ancient ancestors, too, recognized the power of the stars.

Scientists have come to believe that life on earth began around 2,500,000,000 B.C. The first single-celled organisms, ancient ancestors of blue-green algae, developed the ability to change sunlight into energy. The process created life-giving oxygen.

The earliest-known life form in the Southwest, a two-inch-long jellyfish-like creature, was recently dated at 600,000,000 B.C. The fossils were found in 1995, about a hundred miles south of Tucson. As the old Tewa Indian legend explains, these early creatures were "transformed." We call the process evolution.

Natural selection explains how the forces of nature influence the growth and character of the seeds of life. These seeds grow into evolving species. The Pueblo Indians spiritualized these forces of birth and transformation through beings such as *Mui-aingwa*, the spirit of germination, who created life from the earth. *Mui-aingwa* united with *Maasaw*, the spirit of the earth and fire, who is guardian of land, life, and death. Joined with water and air, these were the basic ingredients for life.

The Paleozoic Era, or Age of Fishes, 570,000,000 to 245,000,000 B.C., was a warm, tropical time when mountains rose from the buckling of the Earth. Complex swimming creatures appeared in the waters. The first jawless fish developed in the seas. Land plants attracted the ancestors of the scorpion to crawl from the sea. Insects such as dragon flies appeared, as did the earliest reptiles.

In the lowlands and shallow bays, great limestone beds formed like gigantic coral reefs. That limestone was to became a prized material for building stone houses and carving effigies and spiritual objects of power.

◄ *The Palatki Ruin is set in Red Cliffs, Arizona. The area was occupied by the Water and Cloud Clans.*

Granite came later; the oldest granite in the Southwest, found in Tonto National Monument and Death Valley, dates from around 1,800,000,000 B.C. After the first granite was formed, a billion years of constant erosion created the sand, silt, and clay that became the materials of pottery making.

Around 300,000,000 B.C., the creation of the Grand Canyon began, as land sank throughout the Southwest and waters crept in from the Sea of Cortez in Baja, Mexico. Over millions of years, layer upon layer of silt and microscopic sea creatures piled up under the water and compressed into sedimentary rocks. In some hollows the sediment became more than three miles deep; the layered rock in the bottom of the Grand Canyon is now approximately a thousand feet deep. When the inland sea retreated, the Colorado River began carving the canyon, with the help of the wind and other natural forces. Among the sediments left behind after the retreat of the inland sea were deposits of *kaolin*, a white chalk used by Puebloan artists as a white wash for walls, wedding robes, body paint, and Kachinas.

During the *Triassic* and *Jurassic* "Age of Reptiles and Dinosaurs," 240,000,000 to 138,000,000 B.C., the Southwest looked similar to the Amazon rain forest. Temperatures on the North and South Poles rarely dipped below 50° F and grew even hotter toward the end of the period. The first rare forms of dinosaurs appeared in the Late Triassic, beginning the great family tree of the species whose name means terrible lizard. Among the earliest dinosaurs were the Prosauropods, ancient ancestors of the Saurischia family.

The second main group of dinosaurs were the Ornithischia, ancestors of the famous Stegosaurus. They were the most ancient ancestors of birds, small feathered creatures called *Archaeopteryx lithographica* or "Ancient Wing." Pterodactyls, reptiles with fifty-foot wingspans, also flew over the Southwest during this era.

Colorado fields that are rich in the remains of dinosaurs have revealed evidence of Allosaurus, Ceratosaurus, Camarasaurus, Amphicoelias, Diplodocus, Stegosaurus, and Camptosaurus from the Upper Jurassic. There were no grasslands yet, but during that era the first flowering plants, the angiosperms, appeared to beautify the Earth. Forests of tall conifers and other species rose and created canopies. Later, the remains of those dense forests formed coal beds and oil fields.

Powerful forces deep within the earth caused upheaval. Uplifting formed the granite Rocky Mountains. Giant balloons of molten lava spewed from fissures and volcanoes. Puebloan people consider all mountains sacred; the San Francisco Peaks near Flagstaff are the traditional home of powerful spiritual beings called Kachinas.

As the great inland sea drained into Baja and the Gulf of Mexico, the Colorado River, and the Rio Grande were born from the headwaters of the Rockies. Near the end of the era, massive meteor showers sent balls of fire crashing to the earth from outer space, gouging huge craters.

Dinosaurs roamed throughout the Western Hemisphere, from the Arctic Circle to Antarctica. Meat-eating dinosaurs, including the Lizard King, Tyrannosaurus Rex, roamed the Southwest. It is believed the giant dinosaur devoured its prey after lunging at it, then digging in its sharp claws and teeth. Other large dinosaurs included Diplodocus, Dicraeosaurus, Cetiosauriscus, and the famous Brontosaurus, or Apatosaurus, and the horned Triceratops.

About 100,000,000 B.C., the weather cooled around the world. Large vegetarian dinosaurs were replaced by smaller, more nimble species.

Then, after surviving on earth for one hundred fifty-five million years, dinosaurs began dying out and became extinct mysteriously in 66,000,000 B.C. Birds may be the surviving descendants of dinosaurs. One theory suggests that dinosaurs became extinct after a massive meteorite crashed to earth at what is now Progresso, Mexico, on the Yucatan Peninsula. Scientists estimate the meteorite was six miles wide and traveling at perhaps sixty thousand miles per hour. Violent earthquakes, giant tidal waves, and the dark cloud of dust it created may have choked life from a cold Mother Earth.

Archaeologists believe the first ancestors of humans appeared around 3,750,000 B.C., late in the Tertiary Period of the Cenozoic Era. Dr. Mary D. Leaky and the National Geographic Society found evidence at Laetoeli, Tanzania, in Africa. The oldest fossil remains dated 3,350,000 B.C.

Dr. Donald C. Johanson discovered the three million-year-old remains of a woman called "Lucy" at Hadar, Ethiopia; her Hominid species was named *Australopithecus afarensis*. Two-and-a-half-million-year-old stone tools, similar to Oldowan tools, were discovered in Ethiopia. Two million years ago, a group of families lived in a South African cave. Professor Raymond Ard named their species *Australopithecus africanus*.

During the Tertiary Period, 63,000,000 to 2,000,000 B.C., grasslands grew across the Southwest, transforming the desert into savanna homelands for mammals, including woolly, elephant-like mastodons, miniature horses, wild dogs, and camels. As the Sierra Mountains rose, Pacific storm systems were blocked, creating desert-like conditions. Earthquakes cracked open faultlines two to three hundred miles long. Volcanoes rose and erupted, sending blankets of volcanic ash and rivers of molten lava across the land. Salty lakes, survivors of the great inland sea, became sources of minerals such as borax, saltpeter, sodium carbonate, and the gypsum Puebloan artists later carved for inlaid jewelry.

In the region of the Gila Cliff Dwellings in southwestern New Mexico, two plates of earth crashed together, creating volcanic cones and explosions. Over the next ten million years, volcanic ash and lava piled up more than a thousand feet deep. From headwaters in the Gila Wilderness basin, three branches of the Gila River flowed westward to the Sea of Cortez in Baja California.

As early as 7,000 B.C., the ancient people of this region were using volcanic rock caves and alcoves as shelters. Later those shelters were developed into cliff dwellings.

In Arizona, where Montezuma Castle and Tuzigoot National Monuments are today, the Verde Valley was formed, a natural limestone recess eroded with layers of sandstone, mud, and conglomerate. Earthquake faultlines closed up the valley and created the Verde Lakes. When the natural dams collapsed, waterfalls cascaded down the valley between the Mogollon Rim, the edge of the Colorado Plateau, and the Black Hills Range. The area attracted mastodons, giant cats, camels, and other exotic animals. Intense volcanic activity created cycles of destruction, rebirth, and transformation.

Volcanoes made powerful impressions on the early Southwest people. Stories were passed down describing the creation of mountains, rivers, plants, animals, and people. A constant thread in the stories was the acceptance of the natural law that life is followed by death, creation by destruction, through unending cycles of existence.

Pleistocene - Age of Mammals (2,000,000-10,000 B.C.)

With the onset of the Ice Ages, glaciers ground down the Sierra and the Rocky Mountains, carving valleys into the high deserts of the Southwest. Rain storms filled the rivers and created inland lakes. As the glaciers retreated northward, the desert bloomed with cactus plants, Joshua trees, and other vegetation.

A million years ago, a giant volcano rose and twice erupted in the Jemez Mountains fifteen miles east of Bandelier. Both those eruptions were one hundred times more powerful and destructive than the 1980 eruption of

▲ *The sun sets over the San Francisco Peaks, Homol'ovi State Park, Arizona, called the "Home of the Kachinas."* ▶ *The "Avanyu, Plumed Water Serpent" Petroglyph is near Santa Fe, New Mexico. This Mesoamerican being is believed to live deep within the body of Mother Earth.*

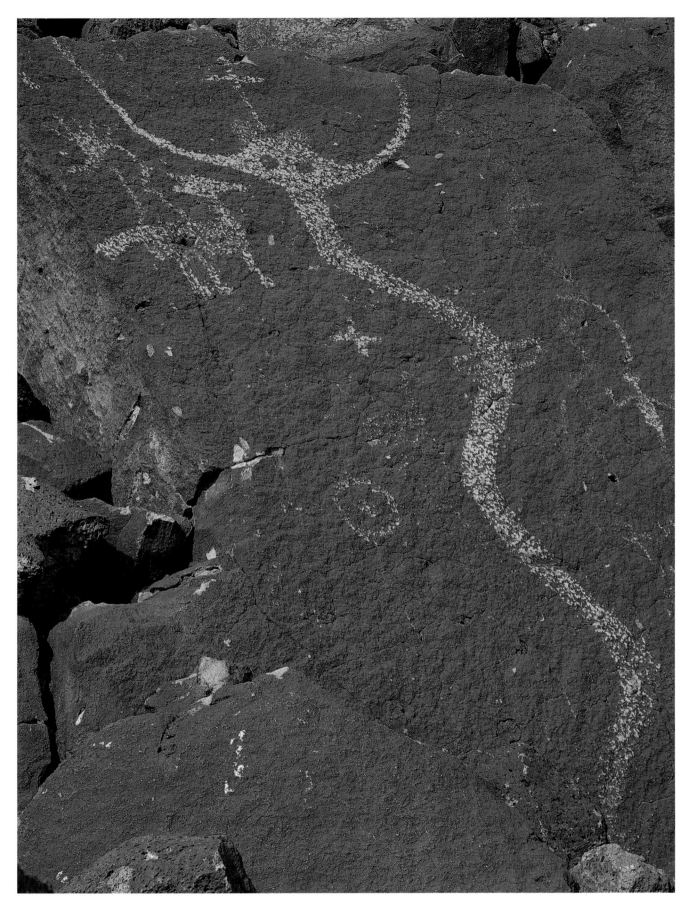

Mt. Saint Helens in Washington State. A river of molten lava charged down Frijoles Canyon, and big, black volcanic clouds rained suffocating ashes all the way to Oklahoma. Later, when ancient ancestors of Pueblo people moved into the area, they found the pink-grey volcanic rock soft enough to carve out cliff dwellings with stone tools.

The oldest evidence of ancient European ancestors is from eight hundred thousand years ago. It was found at Soleihac, in the Massif Central area of France. Evidence indicates that half a million years ago, mammoth elephants were hunted at Ambrona and Torralba northeast of Madrid, Spain. In 400,000 B.C., Homo Erectus walked the beaches on the French Riviera. A hundred thousand years later, people crossed the English channel to settle Britain.

Neanderthal Man appeared around 125,000 B.C. in the Neander Valley near Dusseldorf, Germany. Evidence indicates that relatives of the Neander people later lived in caves in Israel and Iran. Those ancient people sprinkled pollen over the remains of departed loved ones, a religious ritual practiced by some Pueblo Indians.

Most Native Americans reject evidence that their origins were anywhere but in the Western Hemisphere. They do not believe their ancient ancestors crossed the Bering Straits into North America. Some jest their ancestors "walked backwards" across the Straits just to fool the archaeologists—the original Native American joke!

One fact remains. The more exacting scientific searching and dating methods become, the further the date of human habitation in this hemisphere is pushed back in time. L. S. Cressman suggests humans lived in the Western Hemisphere as early as 68,000 B.C. Recent studies in the Brazilian Amazon may place the date even earlier.

Paleolithic Period (47,000 - 7,000 B.C.)

In the Southwest, the Paleolithic Period began with a bang. Around 47,000 B.C.—about the time *Homo Sapiens*, the modern human species, emerged—a giant meteor crashed to earth. Traveling at forty-five thousand miles per hour and weighing millions of tons, it landed with a force equal to fifteen million tons of TNT. It created a gaping chasm 570 feet deep, nearly a mile across, and over three miles in circumference. Meteor Crater is seventy miles south of Hopiland, between Flagstaff and Winslow.

At that time, according to archaeologist Pedra Furada and Niede Guidon of the Institute of Advanced Social Science in Paris, people already were living in rock shelters and caves in northeastern Brazil. They painted the walls of their dwellings with images of deer, birds, armadillos, stick figure people, hunting, sex, and childbirth.

◄ ▲ *Yucca, Canyonlands National Park, Utah. Yucca fiber is used in weaving and in sandal making; the roots make soap.*
◄ *Yucca sandals, circa A.D. 100 to 400, are the oldest type of shoe in the Southwest; Edge of the Cedars State Park, Utah.*

The earliest evidence of human habitation in the Southwest, dated at 38,000 B.C., was discovered by archaeologist Richard MacNeish at Orogrand Cave in southern New Mexico. He found a bone spearhead embedded in the toe bone of a Paleolithic species of miniature horse that later became extinct. There were human fingerprints in the clay near a fireplace.

Radiocarbon dating of ancient fire pits indicates that in 35,000 B.C. humans lived near what is now Lewisville, Texas. By 31,000 B.C., people had settled at Monte Verde and west of the Andes in South America, in what is now southern Chile. Wooden artifacts, digging sticks, mortars, spear tips and building foundations have been discovered, preserved under a peat bog. Sixty-five medicinal and herbal plants also were found.

Around 30,000 B.C., Ice Age people were hunting at Kostienki along the Dan River in Siberia. They lived in homes made of mammoth tusks, bones, and hides, and they carved tools and ornaments.

An ancient cooking hearth was found off the Pacific Coast of Santa Barbara on Santa Rosa Island, with the charcoal remains of dwarf mammoths. Jacques Cinq-Mars of the Archaeological Survey of Canada reported finding chipped mammoth bones in the Bluefish Caves and Old Crow Basin in the Yukon, Alaska. Carbon dating indicates people were living around an ancient lake near Tule Springs, Nevada, in 21,800 B.C. and near Valsequillo, Mexico, by 20,000 B.C. Around that time, Cro-Magnon people in Europe began using spear throwers, bone needles, and fishhooks. They made ornaments and musical instruments of bone. People also have lived for eight thousand years, off and on, in *Pikimachay*, Cave of the Fleas, near Ayacucho, Peru, at an altitude of ninety-four hundred feet.

The oldest basket fragments in North America, dated at 17,600 B.C., were found at a rock shelter in southwestern Pennsylvania. The Meadowcroft people, as they are called, also lived in present-day Ohio and West Virginia.

Murals on the walls of Lascaux Cave in Southwestern France date from 13,500 B.C. French connoisseurs consider rock art in their country to be national treasures. Every effort is made to insure not one flake of paint is lost.

By contrast, few of the ancient rock art sites in the Americas are protected. Unfortunately, countless rock art murals in the Southwest have been vandalized by graffiti and gunshots.

Around 13,000 B.C., the global Ice Age began to end. Over the next four thousand years, the giant glaciers retreated and many animal populations thrived, including mammoth, horses, camels, antelope, bison, elk, and deer. Big game hunters followed migrating herds across the Plateau and Great Basin, through the Hovenweep and Mesa Verde areas, over the Rockies, and out across the Great Plains. Melting glaciers caused ocean levels to rise, putting an end to foot travel across the Bering Straits about 10,000 B.C. As the Hopi say, the "back door" was closed.

After 9500 B.C., big game hunters of the Clovis culture hunted mastodons and mammoth elephants with sharp, stone-tipped spears. A sophisticated style of fluted spear point called "Clovis" was found at Llano Estaciado, a mammoth kill site near Clovis, New Mexico. Hunters killed nine woolly mammoths along the San Pedro River at the Lehner Kill Site in southern Arizona.

Groups of extended families lived in the Ventana Cave periodically over the next ten millennia. They used spears for hunting and employed grinding stones to make meal from natural grains.

By 9000 B.C., as the last glacier retreated northward, Clovis hunting groups began to disappear and the Folsom culture emerged. During the next two thousand years, rainfall diminished. Desert lakes shrank, springs dried up, and plants, animals, and people migrated to the wettest locations for survival. Many Pleistocene species were endangered, and some even became extinct. The mammoth, mastodon, saber tooth tiger, woolly rhinoceros, giant sloth, camel, and miniature horse were no more.

Around 8000 B.C., some people took refuge in Sandia Cave, near Albuquerque. Other groups settled at Hopiland.

Post Pleistocene/Archaic Period (7000 - 2000 B.C.)

In 7000 B.C., while hunters were stalking game around Chaco Canyon, the seeds of revolution were growing in the South—a revolution that would change the world. It was not a political revolution; it was agricultural.

In the Mexican valley of *Tehuacán*, an ancient ancestor of corn called *teosinte* was being cultivated. In northeastern Mesoamerica, pumpkins and gourds grew. These vegetables—plus the peppers, peanuts, cashews, avocados, beans, vanilla, tomatoes, potatoes, cotton, rubber, and cocoa developed later—would transform the earth.

A new technique, tree ring dating, is helping us learn more about these early settlers of the Southwest. Developed by Charles Ferguson and his colleagues, this technique involves examining cross sections of log beams and measuring the width of the tree rings. Thin rings mean years of drought; fat rings mean years of high rainfall. Now scientists called dendroclimatologists, using this technique, can accurately date events since 6700 B.C.

We can now tell the exact years the first and last logs were cut to build Mesa Verde, Chaco Canyon, or any other site. When a clan history recounts founding a specific village, the story is fit in sequence. Oral history is transformed into documentary history, making the term "prehistory" obsolete. Evidence confirms what Natives have always said: "History began before Columbus!"

Other technologies are helpful in putting pieces of the historical puzzle back together. Carbon-14 dating measures the rate of disintegration of an organic building block in molecular biology. Potassium-argon works similarly. Scores of other methods prove that archaeology and related fields can be enormously helpful to indigenous people who are standing up for their aboriginal rights. Some descendants want their voices heard when decisions are made about the future of ancient pueblos, shrines, and religious sites. A relationship that was once adversarial is growing harmonious for the benefit of our common heritage.

In 5000 B.C., when Zuni, Hopi, Chaco, and other areas were being settled, corn was domesticated in Mexico. Chili was cultivated in Bolivia. Beans had been domesticated in Mesoamerica by 4000 B.C., but were not introduced into the Southwest until 1600 B.C. The first piñon pine trees arrived at this time in the Great Basin and Southwest, providing high protein nuts. In times of drought, mashed pine nuts fed to babies helped them survive.

About 3600 B.C., when Egyptian pyramids were under construction, corn and squash were being cultivated in New Mexico, according to the dating of seeds in Bat Cave. While Europeans were inventing bronze weapons and the Mesomotamians were developing wheels to move armies, agricultural wizards in the Western Hemisphere were more concerned with feeding people and developing trade and commerce. Little evidence of open warfare has been found.

From 3200 to 2700 B.C., Olmec traders carried on commerce in vegetable seeds, jade, and obsidian throughout Mesoamerica. They constructed stone cities in tropical lowlands and solved problems of periodic droughts by engineering irrigation canals and terraced gardens.

By 3000 B.C., while Eastern Woodland Indians were hammering out copper tools and building birch bark longhouses around the Great Lakes, stone pyramids and religious centers were being built in the South American Andes, at altitudes up to twenty-two thousand feet. Underground pithouses in the Southwest would eventually became ceremonial kivas. Ideas for pyramids and platform religious mounds spread from South to North America, and some were built larger than the Great Pyramids in Egypt. Most indigenous people, however, do not measure their "civilizations" by the size of buildings.

From 2,000 to 1,000 B.C., migrations through the Grand Canyon increased. Zuni Bow and other Cochise Desert culture clans migrated from California and were part of the Mogollon people in central New Mexico. The Hopi Bear Clan migrated into the four directions and reunited in the North before returning through the Grand Canyon. The Spider, Bluebird, and other clans joined them.

These ancient hunters used stone-tipped spears and knives and wore rabbit-fur robes in winter. Artists painted and carved spectacular designs on the canyon walls. Ceremonies were conducted in caves, where caches of ten to twelve miniature twined figurines of deer, and other forms—some with tiny palm-length spears—have been found. These probably were spiritual effigies related to hunting rituals for deer, bighorn sheep, and antelope. Hunting ceremonies were designed to aid in a successful hunt. Hunting bighorn sheep on the narrow trails of the Grand Canyon required skill, courage, and faith.

Forty spirit-like beings painted on a wall in the western part of the Grand Canyon depict bighorn sheep, deer, snakes, and other creatures. Rock art specialist Polly Schaafsma dates them stylistically from 2000 B.C. to A.D. 1. This recently uncovered site is called Shaman's Gallery.

Around 2,000 B.C., the first water wells were dug in the Southwest. This innovation improved water supplies. Ancient ancestors built religions around the two esentials for survival, food and water. Spirituality focused on fertility and relationships with nature, hunting rituals, and agricultural ceremonies from the planting to the harvest.

At this time, the oldest trees in North America, bristlecone pines, were born. Some four-thousand-year-old trees are still alive today. If those trees could talk, they could tell us of remarkable events. Fortunately, we can now learn from their tree rings when the ancient ancestors of the Southwest built their homes, workshops, and places of worship. As we connect stories passed down the generations, the history of the ancient Southwest is coming back to life.

Basketmaker I Period (1000-500/100 B.C.)

Three thousand years ago, long before the first pot was formed, beautiful baskets were woven in the Southwest. Ancient ancestors of master weavers from Hopi, Paiute, Ute, Pima, Papago, and Uto-Aztecan communities divided, and groups migrated from the Great Basin east to the Grand Canyon. Some settled around Chaco Canyon, where basketry and other crafts advanced to a high art.

Beginning around 1000 B.C., when other culture centers were developing around Jemez and Bat Cave in New Mexico, the Mayan city of Nakbe was under construction. Mesoamerican vegetable seeds were spreading throughout the Southwest. By 600 B.C., Mexican beans had been introduced into the Southwest. Technology for large-scale irrigation through river diversion spread into the Southwest from places like the Mayan city of Tikal in Mexico.

Olmec culture flourished at Monte Alban in Mexico; Mixtec jewelry was made of gold, silver, jade, crystal, bone, and turquoise acquired by trade from the American Southwest. The Mayan "City of Kings" was under construction at Copan in Honduras. Cultural exchanges and trade between Mesoamerica and the Southwest influenced people throughout the Western Hemisphere.

Basketmaker II Period (500/100 B.C. to A.D. 400/450)

Introduction of cotton for textiles, development of pottery, and growth in spirituality were features of this period. Clans also united to form tribes. Jemez and Pecos people branched away from the main Tanoan group around 500 B.C. and, in time, developed the distinct Towa dialect. They probably were the Rosa Phase people of the Governador area. Similar unifications occurred among the Keresan, Zuni, Hokan, Athabascan, and Uto-Aztecan speaking peoples.

Cotton and sunflowers, both Mexican imports, have been found at Tularosa Cave and at Snaketown in southern Arizona, dating around 350 B.C. Fine textiles and baskets have been found in caves and rock shelters. Fur robes, exquisite twined bags, and painted cloth were preserved at White Dog Cave in the Kayenta region north of Hopi.

People living in the Hohokam region of southern Arizona and the Mogollon region from New Mexico south began forming clay inside baskets to create pottery around 300 B.C. Hohokam engineers also built irrigation canals along the Gila and Salt Rivers. At that time, fifty families lived year-round at Snaketown in southern Arizona. These Hohokam people also created the first etchings, using plant juice to etch designs into Pacific seashells.

Cultures in the Southwest, as in Mesoamerica, organized spiritually around ceremonial cycles. Mayan astronomers in Mexico developed a written calendar more accurate than any other on earth at that time. The oldest precise date, found on a Mayan monument in the Yucatan by archaeologists from the National Geographic Society, is November 4, 291 B.C. At that time, Olmec culture was flourishing in Central America. High in the Andes in South America, ancient ancestors of the Inca also were developing remarkable cities, cultures, and technologies.

In 200 B.C., cultural characteristics began to identify the people archaeologists called "Anasazi" as a distinct culture. They lived in more permanent dwellings and grew crops. Corn was grown by 185 B.C. near Homol'ovi, a settlement near Winslow, Arizona, south of Hopi. "Anasazi" populations grew steadily, making agriculture increasingly important. Their descendants reorganized into distinct Puebloan communities by the fourteenth century. The Hopi call their ancient ancestors *Hisatsinom*. San Juan Pueblo scholar Alfonso Ortiz says, "The Pueblo people are the only one of the cultural groups identifiable as long ago as two millennia that have survived with clearly unbroken cultural continuity into the last quarter of the twentieth century."

Around A.D. 1, ancestors of the Towa-speaking Jemez settled at Wavinatita, near Dulce, New Mexico. They lived there for the next thirteen hundred years. The Keresan Eastern Ancestral Puebloans of Mesa Verde and Chaco Canyon lived to the west, and the Tewas to the north.

Moche culture in Peru and the Toltecs in Yucatan were flourishing by A.D. 100. Pyramids were built to the sun and moon at Teotihuacán. The Toltecs chose a site near a large volcano. Although living under threat of eruption, they grew wealthy from their extensive trade in volcanic glass. Local craftsmen created sharp obsidian knives, spears, and other tools. The city, then fifty thousand strong, was larger than most in Europe. London was not yet founded, and the population of Paris was scarcely ten thousand.

Southwest potters traded their pottery as far away as Teotihuacán. From 100 to 450, coiled and fired brown pottery was made by the Mesa Verdean, Mogollon, and Hohokam. Black-on-white designs grew in popularity among Mesa Verdean potters. Redware became prominent in Mogollon pottery, and buffware was developed in Hohokam settlements in southern Arizona. The Hohokam also made pottery figurines with spiritual significance for fertility, agricultural productivity, and weather control.

By 300, ancestors of the Keresans, some from the Chaco Canyon area, were developing an elaborate religious and ceremonial system under the guidance of societies of spiritual and medicine leaders. Among their goals were bountiful crops nourished by gentle rains, protection from illness, and harmony with the forces of the universe. Their world views embraced fundamental principles: The universe is an orderly phenomenon. People or things are not merely "good" or "bad." "Evil" is a disturbance in the equilibrium that exists between man and the universe, while "good" is a positive frame of mind or action that maintains harmonious balance.

Tewa scholar Edward Dozier explained:

To keep man and the universe in harmonious balance, all must work together and with "good" thoughts. Unanimous effort of body and mind is not only a key value, but it is also enforced . . . The cacique and the War Captains exert strict control over the activities of village members and see that all physically able members participate in the rigid calendric series of ceremonies.

To keep society in harmony is challenging. Spirituality has always united Pueblo communities. Political alliance developed as a means of survival; it began as resistance against the Spanish invasion, in the Pueblo Revolt of 1680.

Basketmaker III Period (400/450 - 700)

Bows and arrows, spindle whorls for making cotton string, and advancements in textiles and pottery marked this period. Clothing styles featured complex woven and painted designs. Precious materials were imported for inlaid and carved jewelry. Most homes were built underground, cozy rooms insulated by the earth. Houses above the surface were built with hand-shaped stones.

Southwest settlements became more permanent. People were living in pithouses in Chaco Canyon, in places like Shabik'eshchee Village. Deep, circular pithouses were arranged near larger kivas, the underground religious chambers symbolizing the "womb of Mother Earth." Most of the Eastern Keresan kivas were round; those in western Mogollon were rectangular with rounded corners. In the kivas, priests smoked tobacco from cloud-blower pipes, sending forth prayers with the smoke. Ceremonial dancers wore seashell beads and turquoise pendants.

Agriculture grew in importance with increasing populations, favorable rains, and the introduction of a variety of crops. People cultivated more and preserved vegetables by sun drying. Seeds were parched with hot coals, then ground into meal. Large pits were used for food storage. Pottery protected food from moisture, insects, and rodents.

Many of those later called "Anasazi" were Keresan-speaking people. As their population grew, some moved north from Chaco into the Mesa Verde region. The spread of the pottery is evidence of their expansion. Trade routes opened between Chaco, Mesa Verde, Zuni, and Hopi. Villages at Hopi were well established, as their diverse material culture, agriculture, and ceremonies indicate.

While some clans moved from Chaco to Mesa Verde, others moved from Mesa Verde to settle at Hovenweep, where soil was more fertile and vegetation denser. They built villages on the mesa ridges and surrounding flatlands. During this time of diversification, ancient ancestors of the San Juan, Santa Clara, San Ildefonso, Pojoaque, Tesuque, and Nambe people branched out from the main Tanoan group and eventually developed the Tewa dialect.

At a time when condors flew over Tiahuanaco cities around Lake Titicaca in Bolivia, giant spirits with human bodies and bird heads were painted in Canyon de Chelly. Mesoamerican parrots and macaws were raised here, as well as turkeys. Traders brought goods to Canyon de Chelly, Hopi, and Zuni, as well as Chaco and Mesa Verde.

As early as 500, the oldest Hopi village of Shungopavi was settled by the Bear Clan. The Bluebird, Strap, and other groups of extended families followed. Archaeological evidence indicates sites around Hopi may have existed as early as 8,000 B.C. According to oral tradition recorded almost a century ago by Smithsonian anthropologist Walter Jessie Fewkes, Tusayan, now called Hopiland, was founded by three groups of clans led by the *Hanau* Bear Clan, *Tcua* Snake Clan, and *Patun* Squash Clan. The Bear people came from Muiobi in the Rio Grande Valley. The Snake people came from Tokonabi, Navajo Mountain, in Arizona; the Squash people came from the Little Colorado River in the south.

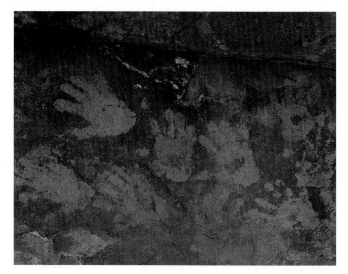

▲ *Handprints grace Horseshoe Ruins, Hovenweep National Monument, Utah. San Juan and Mesa Verde people called it home.* ▶ *Sandstone tableta depicts rainbow, clouds, emergence, flight, and migration symbols at Raven Site, White Mountain Archeological Center, St. Johns, Arizona; circa A.D. 1450.*

Pueblo Life

Pueblo I Period (700 - 900)

This period marks the development of ideas for building communities. Although the origins of community are found farther back in time, the establishment of permanent pueblos changed the course of history in the ancient Southwest. After long migrations, clans found their proper places, which they sometimes referred to as the "Center of the World." Culture centers grew at Hopi, Zuni, Acoma, and Rio Grande Pueblos. Each community needed to decide which new clans would be invited to stay permanently.

Hopi Bluebird Chief Andrew Hermaquaftewa described the arrival of successive clans:

Now when people . . . asked permission to be admitted into the village, the traditional leaders would hold council and consider the question. The newcomers would be asked what could they do by way of helping the Hopi Way of life. The Bluebird Chief must ask them if they have any kind of weapons. All people must leave their weapons of destruction before they would be admitted into the Hopi Village.

The Chief explained their respect for traditional laws and their strong faith in the Earth Spirit, *Maasaw.* A model for right human behavior, he said, was established from the beginning.

◀ *Corn Stalk Petroglyph depicts the symbol of the Corn Clan from the Tewa and Keresan Pueblo near Santa Fe, New Mexico.* ▲ *Mano and matate, shown here with corn in a basket, were tools used for grinding corn into meal at Raven Site, White Mountain Archeological Center, St. Johns, Arizona.*

Boastful people cannot become part of a Hopi Village. Only those who desire to live peacefully, to harm no one, are admitted into the religious order of the village life . . . Here they would receive all their altars and their religious songs from the mother village. Because Maasaw has told us to guard this land by this altar which was set up at Shungopavi, other villages have taken this flower to carry to their village. In this way, they want to live and carry on the duties of all the clan leaders as they were placed upon them by Maasaw.

One of the most important traditions from the beginning to this day is to honor clan responsibilities. Each group of extended families has important spiritual and social roles. When all are honored, society stands in harmony. The Bluebird Chief further explained:

So was the pattern established through which all Hopi villages were built. It was all according to the instructions given by Maasaw. The village leaders are appointed by the proper religious leaders from Shungopavi. They have the same obligations, duties, and authority as the leaders at Shungopavi. Nothing happened by chance. Everything was according to the dictates of Maasaw. Village life was established, leaders were appointed, and different clans were given special duties. The land was being taken care of under the obligations of Maasaw.

Here is a major difference between ancient Southwest and European thinking. The land was not owned privately or by a king. Instead, people were encouraged to be caretakers of the land for the Spirit of the Earth. This fundamental belief was held throughout the Southwest and in many other parts of the Western Hemisphere. Ancient tribal Europe and other parts of the world shared similar Mother Earth religions. We may all find, at our most ancient roots, the beliefs that the Hopi consider universal:

Our religious teachings are based upon the proper care of our land and the people who live upon it. We must not lose the way of life of our religion if we are to remain Hopis, The Peaceful. We believe in that; we live it, day by day. We do not want to give it up for the way of another. For the benefit of our people throughout our land, for the people to come after us in our land, and for those who care to learn we Hopis want to be known among all other people throughout all other lands as the Hopi, the People of Peace. Let all people hear our voice.

Hopi Bluebird Chief Hermaquaftewa explained these teachings before I was born. However, his successor, Earl Pela, repeated the same lessons to me fifteen years ago. Both were spokesmen for the Kikmongwi, the highest spiritual leaders, who are chosen from the Bear Clan. Today, Earl Pela's descendants are holding on to this peaceful way of life. Perhaps, through our better understanding, these living "Anasazi" villages can be recognized as truly sovereign, independent city-states.

From ancient times, spiritual leaders were from the Bear Clan because the bear was respected as the most powerful creature in the Western Hemisphere. Bear imagery has a long history in the Southwest. Bear paw effigies dating from 700 have been found at Tularosa Cave. In the Pueblo spiritual world, bear tracks signify the bear's curing power. From the Hopi to the Keresans of the Rio Grande, bear doctors were said to "become bears."

Snakes are also regarded as powerful beings, messengers to the Earth Spirit. The Hohokam of Snaketown built a major cultural center in Arizona. Their elaborate network of canals irrigated fields for hundreds of miles. They revered the power of the rivers, which they believed embodied the Plumed Water Serpent. This being was said to ". . . know Mother Earth most intimately, for it lives within her bosom." Depictions of the Plumed Water Serpent are found from the Southwest to the pyramids of Mesoamerica.

In 741, one of the largest pyramids in the Western Hemisphere was completed in the Mayan city of Tikal. In 750, when the Mesa Verdean population at Hovenweep had tripled, their cousins to the south learned a hard lesson about growing too big, too rich, too fast. Teotihuacán, in Mexico, which had a population of some 125 thousand people, was attacked and destroyed by a jealous northern rival. The sacred ceremonial center was decimated; the city was abandoned. Some of the refugees may have relocated in the Southwest.

From 800 to 850, during what was called the Hohokam Gila Butte phase, Mesoamerican ball courts were constructed in Arizona. This sport symbolized spiritual beings trying to make the world more harmonious for humans; the game was a microcosm of the cosmos.

Two hundred courts were built over the next three centuries in Arizona; the sport spread all the way to Wupatki, near Flagstaff, by A.D. 1150. The game was played with a small ball on courts built in two sizes: about 50 by 80 feet, or 110 by 200 feet. The object of the game was to get the ball through a hoop mounted vertically on a wall. The players could use only their arms and hips.

At this time, the Zacatecas near Jalisco, Mexico, developed spiritual societies which involved kachina-like portrayal of spiritual deities. The object was to become one with particular spirit beings. Among the Hohokam, the members sometimes were plumed with Macaw parrot tail feathers, as Hopi and some Puebloan dancers are today.

The Zacatecas spoke a Tepehuan language related to the language of the Aztecs, Pimas, and Hopi; the trade route from Mexico to Arizona also represented a chain of dialects in a common language corridor. The Zacatecas constructed new spiritual centers at Alta Vista, so they could have carried new spiritual ideas and ritual objects, such as iron-pyrite mirrors and Kachina-like designs, to Arizona.

Kokopelli, the Humpbacked Flute Player, also appeared in Hohokam and Mogollon art. Near Phoenix, large figurines of Flute Players with long feathers in their hair were found in a cache from this period. Flute ceremonies were related to corn and the distribution of agricultural seeds. Flute figurines were buried with the dead in elaborate rituals. The music of *Kokopelli* grows stronger to this day. The corn he carried on his back now helps feed the world.

Pueblo II Period (900 - 1100/1150)

This was an age of great migrations. More than two hundred clans continued their quest for the center of the world, their destined place. Some found what they were seeking at Zuni, Acoma, Hopi, and the Rio Grande Valley.

Although the precise date is debatable, the Kiowa-Tanoan people of the Northern Plains moved southward through Wyoming and Colorado. The main group divided in two; the Kiowa moved to Oklahoma, while the Tanoans moved toward the Rio Grande Valley.

Some Tanoan speakers migrated briefly to Mesa Verde before moving toward the Rio Grande. Ancestors of Taos, Picuris, Sandia, and Isleta—Tiwa speakers of the Tanoan language—settled in the Rio Grande Valley. Evidence of their migration is found in their beautiful black-on-white pottery that is found from San Juan and Mesa Verde down the Rio Grande Valley. Some of the clans stayed to help build Chaco and Mesa Verde. Other clans led the way to their present pueblos.

Tewa scholar Alfonso Ortiz from San Juan Pueblo recounted the contributions of his ancestors:

> In their [Pueblo people's] greatest time, from the tenth through the thirteenth centuries, they built and occupied the great architectural wonders at Chaco Canyon, Mesa Verde, Casa Grande, and numerous other places spread out over what are now five large states.

The Tewa settled the rich Rio Grande Valley and the mountain country between Santa Fe and Jemez.

▲ *Silica-bearing ground waters seeped through logs two hundred million years ago, changing living trees to petrified wood, Petrified Forest National Park, Arizona.* ▶ *A late spring snowstorm covers Tsegi Canyon, homeland of the Snake, Horn, and Badger Clans, Navajo National Monument, Arizona.*

Tewa tradition describes the founding of ten villages near Posipopi, Ojo Caliente, eighteen miles northwest of San Juan. At the hot springs, mineral water bubbles from the ground at 90 to 122° F. The greenish pool is one of Tewa's most sacred places. They believe legendary Tewa culture hero *Posejumu* once lived there, and that his spirit returns each year to visit the spirit of his grandmother.

To escape another powerful spirit serpent, the people then resettled in seven communities: San Juan, Santa Clara, San Ildefonso, Nambe, Tesuque, Pojoaque, and Jacona. Other temporary settlements also were founded, but, like Jacona, were later abandoned. People migrated to the east and west sides of the Rio Grande and created summer and winter moieties. Archaeological studies of pottery, Tewa oral history, and nineteenth-century studies by Bandelier and others validate this traditional interpretation of Tewa migrations into the Rio Grande Valley.

According to San Ildefonso tradition, Tewa ancestors living north of Mesa Verde migrated south to the Pajarito Plateau, founding two villages, Potsuwi (Otowi) and Tsankawi. They settled at their present pueblo around the beginning of the twelfth century.

During the 1920s, Elsie Parsons recorded this migration story told by a San Juan elder:

Migration: *The Boy Who Broke His Fast*

Oweweham'baiyo lived at Uwipinge . . . The people had moved along Pingkwaiye (Sangre de Cristo Mountains behind Santa Fe). The eastern mountains belonged to the Winter People [Tanoan moiety or group of clans] and the western mountains belonged to the Summer People. Those on the Eastern Mountains, the Winter People, were eating deer, elk (the meat of wild animals); and the Summer People were eating jucca [yucca] fruit (pahbe), mantsanitabe (apples?), berries (puhpahbe), prickly pear (saebe)—all different kinds of fruit.

The Winter People's leader was Oyk'ke, the Summer People's leader was Poaetoyo. As they were walking divided, some on the west side liked the east side and walked over, some on the east side liked the west side and walked over. All came down there to Uwipinge. So when they were all down together, they talked about where they were going to make a place to live. So they said, "From here we ought to find a place to live, wherever we like."

Some said, "We like Oke'anybu."

So they said, "Then you will be Oké (San Juan)."

Others said, "We like to be on the other side of the river." So they gave them a name, Kahpo, Leaf Water (Santa Clara).

So others said, "We like that place on the other side of the river." So they gave them the name Pow`oge (San Ildefonso).

Others said, "We like the same river, clear up there, Kibu` (gopher place)."

"Well, you have the name Nambé."

Others said, "We like way up there, Tatunge, dry ones."

"You have the name T'et'suge (Tesuque)."

The people from down there, they always like to drink water. "So you have the name Posuwege (Pojoaque)." These six have just one language [Tewa].

We used to live at Okeowingeanyebu [a San Juan ruin at Sunflower Corner, on the west side of the Rio Grande, five miles north of the Chama River fork]. So they said, "Here we do not have a good life. Let us go over to Okeowinge powongwi koochute. At Okeowinge powongwi koochute at that time it was new."

The story offers a traditional Tewa rationalization for their migrations—the search for "a good life." People around the world could give the same reasons.

Chaco Canyon pueblos were constructed around 900. Uto-Aztecan speakers hold a tradition of living at Chaco. Keresan-speaking people also lived around Chaco, Aztec Ruins, and present-day Bloomfield. The Keresans held the Corn Dance and had special knowledge about the powers of bears. In the late 1200s, the Keresans migrated southward, down the valleys of the Rio Grande and Rio Puerco.

Population increased at Chaco Canyon, and construction began at Pueblo Bonito, Penasco Blanco, and Una Vida. Some pithouses were still in use. According to oral history, certain Zuni clans migrated up the Colorado and Rio Puerco Rivers to Chaco. There was active trade in pottery, turquoise, and other goods. Eighty percent of the pottery found at Chaco was from trade.

During the 900s, building techniques at Mesa Verde, Chaco, and other related communities became more sophisticated. Sandstone masonry was developed. Kivas were expanded into a keyhole shape with the addition of a small room to the south or southeast. Chaco Canyon residents began to compete with the Hohokam for the allegiance of the people living between their cultural centers. Networks of exchange were restructured. The Hohokam may have developed a moiety social structure similar to those in the Rio Grande pueblos, with villages divided into summer and winter groups. The groups alternated governing responsibility during the two halves of the year. Duality symbols appeared as alternating motifs on pottery, in east-west ball courts, and in community houses and kivas.

Around 1000, Hopi and Acoma Pueblos were growing. Hopi *Tcua* Snake, *Toho* Puma, *Huwi* Dove, *Ucu* Cactus, *Yunu* Opuntia Cactus, and *Ala* Horn Clans migrated to the Hopi mesas in Arizona. They came from Tokonave or Tokonabi, Navajo Mountain, near the juncture of the Little Colorado and the Great Colorado River in southern Utah. The two largest pueblos were Betatakin and Keet Seel.

Another group of clans soon arrived at Hopi, led by the *Patun* Squash people from the Little Colorado River. Three

◄ *Sunrise shows aligned doorways in Pueblo Bonito at Chaco Culture National Historic Park, New Mexico. Chaco was occupied circa A.D. 900 to 1150.*

other clans came with them: *Atoko* Crane, *Kele* Pigeon-hawk, and *Tubic* Sorrow-making. They originally settled on Second Mesa at Tcukubi. Later, some moved to Old Mishongnovi, others to Awatovi, and some to Walpi. The *Ala* Horn Clan arrived, along with the *Lenya* Flute Clan. The clans from Tokonabi brought with them the *Tcua-wimpkias* Snake Society, the *Tcub-wimpkias* Antelope Society, and special knowledge of the power of bears.

On July 5, 1054, people around the world looked to the heavens as a brilliant supernova exploded, producing the Crab Nebula. The exploding star was so bright and large, people could see it in the daytime for three weeks. It was visible at night for two years. From Mexico to northern Arizona and Chaco Canyon in New Mexico, the event was recorded in pictographs and petroglyphs, with the exploding star correctly positioned near the tip of a crescent moon on the horizon.

The message from the sky was followed, in 1064, by one from the earth. Sunset Crater volcano erupted sixty miles southwest of Hopi pueblos, raining ashes all the way to Oklahoma.

In 1066, Haley's Comet streaked across the sky. Then, on March 7, 1076, a total solar eclipse darkened the daytime sky south of Chaco Canyon and cut a large swath across the Southwest. Soon after, five astronomical observatories were constructed at Chaco, and others rose throughout the Southwest. The astronomical events may have influenced ancient priests to connect ceremonial cycles with solar, lunar, and stellar cycles.

The construction boom that followed these events included the creation of Pueblo Bonito and the greatest architectural achievements in the ancient Southwest.

Pueblo III Period (1100/1150-1300)

This cycle in Pueblo history began with a burst of creative expression and ended after a devastating drought. It demonstrates the courage and determination of the Pueblo people when faced with adversity and diversity. The arrival of so many different clans, societies, and tribes challenged people's tolerance. Philosophies, visionary movements and religions from far away arrived by the trade routes. Internal and external forces challenged each community. Like their ancient ancestors, many people were forced to walk away from their greatest material creations, pueblos constructed over generations. However, they carried within themselves something more important than material things—their spirituality and family histories.

In 1100, Chaco Canyon was at its zenith, growing as distant clans arrived. Pueblo Bonito expanded to eight hundred rooms and rose five stories high, surrounding large plazas and Great Kivas. Complex road systems were built. Copper bells, shell beads, conch shell trumpets, and live macaw parrots came by trade from Mesoamerica. Turquoise from Cerrillos and other sites was traded as far as South America.

Powerful religious ideas spread by word of mouth throughout the Western Hemisphere. Members of the Kachina Society describe two main groups of Kachinas, the Creator's helpers. One group has ancient roots in the Southwest. The other traces its origins to Mexico, Mesoamerica, and South America. In time, the two groups drew together through shared faiths.

According to oral traditions, the oldest Kachinas were present at the emergence into the Fourth World. Others came from the south and spread from pueblo to pueblo. Early Mimbres pottery from southern New Mexico depicted a host of Kachina-like figures and supernatural beings, humans, and animals. Mogollon rock art reflects this spiritual tradition that may be related to the development of the Kachina societies.

Kachina Society members from the Rio Grande Valley moved westward to Hopiland and founded the villages of Kicu and Winba or Katcinaba, three miles east of Sikyatki, a Hopi pueblo on First Mesa. They later spread to Walpi and other main villages. The Kachina and *Anwuci* Crow clans carried with them two important ceremonies, the *Powamu* Bean Dance and the *Niman* Home Dance.

Wooden spiritual artifacts from Chetro Ketl in Chaco Canyon reveal information about varieties of Kachinas and their characteristics. Among the artifacts was a lightning lattice similar to one now carried by Lightning Man in the spring fertility *Powamu* ceremony. It was identified by a delegation of Hopi elders. Kachina spiritual societies still exist at Hopi, Zuni, and Rio Grande pueblos.

By 1100, population had increased along the Little Colorado River, a staging area for clans requesting entrance to Hopi. Kayenta and Mogollon of Sinagua were living in the Homol'ovi region near Winslow. They used sandstone hoes to cultivate Mesoamerican cotton, important for weaving Kachina textiles, capes, robes, kilts, belts, and sashes worn by dancers.

Sometime during this period, small groups of Athabascan-speaking people from the Northwest began to arrive in the Southwest. They were the ancient ancestors of the Diné Navajo and Apache people. They arrived gradually in small groups, occupied areas abandoned by Puebloan people, and learned Pueblo weaving techniques.

Between 1100 and 1150, while the Toltecs in Mexico and the Cahokia people on the Mississippi River were building huge pyramids, major changes were occurring in the Southwest. A group of spiritual priests and civic leaders migrated from Mexico into Arizona, centering in Hohokam communities in the Phoenix Basin, and in the Gila, Verde, and Salt River Valleys. Death rituals changed. Artistic design symbols of lizards, snakes, quail, and water birds were replaced with toads, frogs, and raptorial birds. Hohokam builders adopted a new architectural style. The southern sport of the ball game ended. Clay censers, stone bowls, and paint palettes disappeared. Platform mounds were enlarged and became dominant features of communities.

Important status symbols included nose and lip plugs of argillite and other fine materials. The "pipette" symbol on Southwest rock art paralleled the Mesoamerican Water God, *Tlaloc*.

A crisis soon occurred in Hohokam communities; in 1130, a drought began, lasting fifty years. Chaco Canyon suffered. The soil became encrusted with alkali, animals began to move away, firewood and logs for construction became depleted, and the Chaco social structure began to wane. People moved away.

Snaketown and other villages along the Salt River and other valleys were abandoned. Around 1125, Sinagua farmers moved from the Sunset Crater area to the Verde Valley. Hohokam lookouts sighted northerners coming from Sinagua territory. Some were accepted at Tuzigoot, while others went on to Montezuma's Castle. Stone masons united to build two-story, pueblo-style homes.

By 1150, the Chaco complex had collapsed. People settled temporarily with their cousins at Aztec. At Hovenweep in Southeastern Utah, Anasazi architects and engineers began supervising construction of larger Mesa Verde–style pueblos. Their towers served as astronomical observatories. Hopi and other Puebloan priests still track the path of the sun through notches carved into portals through the tops of kivas, aligned with *Tawa*, the sun, as well as Pliades, Orion, and other constellations.

Mesa Verde grew as Chaco declined. According to oral history tradition, Mesa Verde was built by a united effort of the Bear, Antelope, Water, Cloud, Corn, Eagle, Sun, Turkey, Badger, Butterfly, and Parrot Clans. Their clan symbols are found on sandstone mesa walls. Living descendants are found at pueblos throughout Arizona and New Mexico.

But by 1299, Mesa Verde was abandoned forever. The last Mesa Verde chief, according to Badger Clan history, was named *Salavi*, meaning "Spruce." Traditional stories describe how this respected chief sent his people away in search of better land, even though he was too old to travel with them.

Pueblo IV Period (1300 - 1700)

This era marked the period of final unification. Many of the ancient sites were abandoned. The people who built them did not disappear; they moved and regrouped.

In 1299, rains began falling after the long drought. Clans scattered in search of new homelands. Kachina societies throughout the Pueblo world danced and sang in gratitude. Seventy-six Kachina masks—including Maasaw, Tawa, Giant Ogre, Mudhead, Sio Shalako, Tsakwaina, and some warrior Kachinas—were painted in rock art around Homol'ovi, as well as on Hopi pottery. Most Homol'ovi rock art Kachina masks are round or rectangular with small dot eyes and headgear. Some have bared teeth.

An "artistic explosion" occured at Hopi. Black-on-white pottery was replaced by polychrome wares with brilliant black-on-orange, followed by black-on-yellow. With the addition of red and stylized pictorial design elements such as butterflies, parrots, feathers, and waves, Sikyatki Polychrome was born.

Keresan speakers moved from Bandelier to establish Cochiti and San Felipe Pueblos. Related *Hanu* Santa Ana people, San Juan Anasazi, migrated from Aztec and other Four Corners communities to the Rio Grande. Between 1300 and 1425, the main group settled and built Paak'u Pueblo west of the Sandia Mountains near Albuquerque. Another group migrated for a century, living in six villages and two camps before returning, about 1420, to Paak'u.

Towa ancestors of the Jemez and Pecos abandoned settlements in the Gallina area, the site of famous cylindrical towers. Some settled in the mountains and on the mesas around Jemez, west of Santa Fe; others settled in Pecos and the Galisteo region, extending south to Glorieta.

When the Jemez people, who were related to the Kokop Fire Clan group, came to Hopi, they exchanged certain spiritual traditions. The Hemis (Jemez) gave the Kachina mask with the tableta on top in exchange for Hopi masks, which were taken back to Jemez. The Hopi also may have given the Jemez the Snake Society. The Jemez still retain twenty-three religious societies related to fertility (including the Clowns), medicine, hunting, rain, weather control, and war.

According to tradition, the San Ildefonso ancestors migrated south from Potsuwi, Otowi, and Tsankawi villages at the Pajarito Plateau. They later moved southward to found their present pueblo north of Santa Fe. At Pojoaque, sixteen miles north of Santa Fe, a Tewa community built a complex irrigation system for farming. Around 1300, Arroyo Hondo and Pindi Pueblos near Santa Fe were founded. Arroyo Hondo was abandoned in 1350 and reestablished from 1375 to 1425.

The southern Tiwa community of Sandia, fifteen miles north of Albuquerque, was established and making pottery by 1425. They developed a relationship with Hopi, where many moved after the Pueblo Revolt of 1680. Sandia People, with other Rio Grande Pueblo refugees, reportedly walked to Hopi and founded the village of Payupki on Second Mesa. Most returned later to the Rio Grande.

A permanent pueblo was built at Taos, as thirty-two clans organized around six religious societies. The pueblo's traditional name means "at red-willow canyon mouth."

One of the oldest well-dated ceramics of a horn mask with rounded eyes and a small toothed mouth is a Kachina mask painted on pottery from Pot Creek Pueblo near Taos, dated 1325. Figures painted on pottery at Pot Creek pottery have the small toothed mouth that resembles Hopi *Tsakwaina, He'e'e Warrior, Soyoko Ogre*, and *Horo Mana* (Cold Bringing Woman).

Between 1325 and 1490, Rio Grande Kachinas were depicted at Pottery Mound, forty five miles southwest of Albuquerque. There, fifteen to twenty Kachinas have been identified among the numerous star-faced beings, warriors, and snake beings portrayed in pottery and rock art. Star Kachinas were painted on clay pipes at Pecos and on pottery along the Little Colorado River.

Around 1350, a *Hanu* Santa Ana group resettled across the Rio Jemez from the Jemez community of Tsiiyame. The Hanu built Twiiste Puu Tamaya Pueblo and planted corn and squash along the river. When Jemez women crossed the river to help in the corn grinding, some Jemez men became jealous and conspired with Diné Navajo warriors to attack the Hanu. Tradition says the Diné Navajo "had recently arrived in the region."

The Hanu spread piñon sap on their homes and set their own village ablaze, fleeing southward and leaving behind an elderly woman and her great-great grandson. She managed to keep the newborn baby alive by feeding him milky ground piñon nuts. She lived long enough to raise the boy to young adulthood. Then, around 1390, he journeyed southward and was reunited with his mother and family, who had resettled at Kwiiste Kene'ewa on the Rio Puerco.

During the mid-fourteenth century, the ancestors of the San Juan, Santa Clara, San Ildefonso, Nambe, Tesuque, and Pojoaque people left the main Tanoan group and, in time, developed the Tewa dialect.

Also during this period, the Tiwa-speaking people divided; the Taos and Picuris people settled in northern New Mexico, and the Sandia and Isleta settled in the south.

In 1356 and 1382, the Salt and Gila Rivers flooded, destroying Hohokam canal systems. According to stories told by the Water Clan, the floods caused unrest. During that time, they say, the people revolted against elite civil leaders who were living at large platform mounds.

The Water Clan personified the force of the river as the spirit of Palulukon, the Plumed Water Snake, known along the Rio Grande as *Avanyu*. This supernatural being, perhaps related to a Mesoamerican spirit, was described as "the genius of fructification . . . a great crested serpent with mammae, which are the source of the blood of all the animals and of all the waters of the land."

From their town, Kunchalpi, in the Palatkwabi region of the Salt River and Hopi, the Water people stopped periodically six times: at Utcevaca, Kwinapa, Jettipehika or Chaves Pass, Homol'ovi near Winslow, Sibabi near Comar Spring, and finally at Pakatcomo, four miles from Walpi on First Mesa at Hopi. The Water people eventually resettled at Walpi and on Second Mesa.

The Sun Forehead Clan also came from Palatkwabi, but they believe the location was in Mexico at a place of "red rocks." According to a Sun Forehead Clan leader, their ancestors were warriors of the Eagle Clan people who agreed to assume responsibility for conducting the Snake Dance. When the Shungopavi Kikmongwi led them into the pueblo, their clan name was changed from Eagle to Sun Forehead, as a remembrance of the hot sun shining down at that moment on their foreheads.

Around 1400, the Badger Clan moved from a spring, Kisiu-va, high in the Mountains of the Kachinas, to the San Francisco Peaks near Flagstaff. A Kachina Clan also lived there. The Badger people established a village at Tuwanacabi, north of Hopi. From there they wandered to Oraibi Wash where they built a village, the ruins of which are called Siu-va, after a nearby spring. After the Badger people settled at Oraibi, one of their women married a Walpi man, establishing the clan at First Mesa.

When the Hopi village of Awatovi was destroyed because of spiritual corruption, the Badger Clan women also were accepted at Second Mesa. One Kachina figure painted in the Awatovi kiva murals, which may date from the late 1300s, is similar in style to Rio Grande Kachinas on Pottery Mound pottery painted between 1325 and 1490. The evidence of Kachina Society connections between Arizona and New Mexico is clear.

Kachina figures also were painted in kiva murals at pueblos along the Little Colorado River. Kayenta and Mogollon of Sinagua were living in the Homol'ovi area. By the late fourteenth century, their populations had decreased until pueblos were abandoned. Their clans moved to Hopi, Zuni, and Pecos. Around this time, about 1400, a multi-storied pueblo was being constructed around a central plaza at Pecos.

During the fifteenth century, life began to change. The ancient trade network collapsed, ending distribution of seashells from the Gulf of California to the Southwest. Mesoamerican trade also slowed. Mayans abandoned pyramids in Guatemala. Aztecs suffered social upheavals.

Prophecies circulated foretelling the arrival of strangers from afar. The lives of people throughout the Western Hemisphere were about to be turned upside down.

▲ *Traditional human hair belt and braided yucca rope are displayed at Edge of the Cedars State Park, Utah.* ▶ *Sunrise, Pueblo del Arroyo, Chaco Culture National Historic Park, New Mexico. This area was occupied by clans and societies who measured the point of each sunrise for the ceremonial cycle.*

Ancient Peoples of Arizona

Grand Canyon National Park
(Circa 8000 B.C. to present)

For ancient peoples, the Grand Canyon was one of the most sacred sites in the Southwest. It was the place of birth and death, emergence and transformation, the beginning and the end. Some of the most holy shrines were created in its hundreds of caves and outcroppings.

A ninety-year-old Indian grandmother recalled for me her farthest journey west.

I ran right up to the edge of the Grand Canyon, stretched my arms out, tipped my head back and felt the wind blow through my hair. It was at that moment I understood the true meaning of being free . . . like an eagle.

Grandma was blind when she told me her story, but she could see the goodness inside people, and she was proud to be free.

The Zuni called the Grand Canyon the "Place of Beginning," *Chimik'yana'kya deya.* Oral tradition describes the bottom of the Grand Canyon as the spiritual place where ancient Zuni ancestors emerged into this world. The meaning within the story reminds the Zuni that all land and life were born from the Earth Mother.

Ancient Hopi ancestors also emerged from the bottom of the Grand Canyon into the Fourth World, which they called *Tuwaqachi,* "World Complete." A small hole hidden inside their kivas, called the *Sipapu,* symbolizes their connection with Mother Earth and the origins of their birth. Hopi priests make annual migrations back to the Grand Canyon, renewing their living traditions.

The earliest evidence of human life in the Grand Canyon is radiocarbon dated about 8000 B.C.

Around 1000 B.C., Uto-Aztecan groups were migrating around the Grand Canyon. Traditional Hopi stories say that a powerful *Hognyam* Bear Clan migrated from the Rio Grande to Colorado, then southwest to the Colorado River Valley. The Bow and Bear Clans were the first to arrive at Hopiland, and only they were allowed to be *Kikmongwi* or head spiritual leaders. Images of Hopi *Mongkohu,* the high spiritual leaders' crooked canes, are painted on the Canyon walls. These are considered important power objects.

◄ *Sunrise, Mather Point, Grand Canyon. The Canyon has been occupied since 2100 B.C. by Pueblo and Hokan people who spread throughout the Southwest to California and Baja. Evidence indicates human presence as early as 8000 B.C.*

After the Bear people, the next clans to arrive at Hopi were led by the *Tsugnyam* Snake people. Snake symbols also appear in Shaman's Gallery. It is believed these people came from Mohave, up the Colorado River, through the Grand Canyon, and west 125 miles, to where Navajo National Monument is today. Their path became a major trade route for Pacific seashells and other goods. The Hopi, their Uto-Aztecan cousins, the Papago, and the Hokan-Yuman people of Mohave share similar stories of a culture hero who made ritual journeys down the Colorado River to the Pacific for salt and seashells. When the Hopi travel to the bottom of the Grand Canyon for salt, they continue a tradition of carving their clan symbols at a sacred site. Locations of shrines and other sacred sites remain confidential, out of respect for traditional spiritual peoples.

Beginning around 600 or 700, the Cohonina culture, perhaps ancient ancestors of some Havasupai, settled on a plateau south of the Grand Canyon. They moved away during the period from 1050 to 1200.

For more than six centuries, Ancestral Puebloan people migrated up and down the Little Colorado River within the Grand Canyon. Between 1000 and 1100, these people lived at hundreds of sites on the South Rim and deep within the canyon. Their culture is called Kayenta Anasazi; their pottery is Tusayan style, the old provincial name for Hopiland. They farmed all the way up to the high Kaibab Plateau. They encountered the Cohonina, who probably were Hokan-speaking people. The Hopi called them *Supai* and have a *Supai* Kachina.

Some Cohoninas returned after 1300 to gather and hunt on the plateau south of the Grand Canyon, while farming during the summers in Cataract Creek Canyon. These probably were ancient ancestors of the Havasupai.

Almost half a millennium later, in 1869, explorer John Wesley Powell began his journey down the Colorado River into the Grand Canyon. This experience is reenacted annually by people who are venturesome enough to brave the rapids. Others mount burros or horses and trust their mounts to carry them down a narrow trail to the bottom of the canyon.

The Havasupai, a sovereign Indian nation, still hold legal jurisdiction to their reservation here. Visitors who act respectfully are welcome and introduced to the beautiful Havasupai basketry tradition. Today, the Grand Canyon is designated a World Heritage Site.

Casa Grande "Grand House" Ruins National Monument
(Circa 1350-1450)

Casa Grande, the Classic Hohokam "Grand or Great House" between Phoenix and Tucson, was built around 1350 by Hohokam peoples, in a monumental form influenced by Mesoamerican traditions. Like its namesake, the Casas Grandes in Chihuahua, it was an important center for trade between Mexico and the Southwest.

The walls of this Casa Grande, made of a mixture of clay and cement-like caliche, are four stories high and nearly two feet thick. The compound was surrounded by a high adobe wall. In a Mesoamerican-style ball court two hundred yards away, hundreds of spectators watched players compete to get the ball through a vertical hoop. The game was popular throughout Mexico and Central America.

The dominant language of this region was Uto-Aztecan, a family of dialects spoken by local *Tohono O'odham* Papago and Pima people. Related languages range from Hopi in the north to Aztec in the south. Some Casa Grande people may have been ancient ancestors of the *Patki* Water Clan, as well as Young Corn, Cloud, Tadpole, Frog, Snow, Rabbit, Rabbitbrush, Tobacco, Parrot, Kachina, Snake and Sun Forehead Clans. They recount relationships with other Hohokam settlements at Montezuma's Castle in the Verde Valley, Snaketown in the Gila River Valley, and perhaps Homol'ovi along the Little Colorado River. Their oral history tradition suggests they originated in Mexico, a place of red rocks called, in Hopi, *Palatkwabi.*

These people have at least one thing in common. They were survivors of floods. This may be why Casa Grande was built a safe distance from the Gila River. The Hohokam also were master canal builders, constructing a network over two hundred fifty miles long. The main line of the Casa Grande canal system fed in safely sixteen miles upriver. The people respected the power of the rivers, described in spiritual terms as the giant Horned or Plumed Water Serpent. Descriptions parallel those of the southern *Quetzalcoatl,* the god of life and fertility, and *Tlaloc,* deity of rain and thunder, and *Avanyu* or *Palulukon* in the north. Hopi Snake dancers paint an image of the Water Serpent on their kilts, as do some Rio Grande Pueblo Buffalo dancers. Their ceremonies are intended to control rains, lightning, thunder, snow, hail, and floods.

Casa Grande was constructed during the height of the Nahuatl-Aztec power in Mexico. The Great House was abandoned a century later, about 1450, when the Aztec Empire was beginning to crumble. These parallel events may offer clues for solving the two mysteries: Who lived at Casa Grande? Why did they leave?

Some believe this was the home of a powerful group of priests. Excavations around Casa Grande revealed masterful jewelry, including seashell and thunderbird pendants inlaid with turquoise and precious stone mosaic. This style is still produced by Keresan artists at Santo Domingo in New Mexico and traded to Hopi and other Pueblo dancers, who wear them as centerpieces for their traditional regalia.

From the year one to about 1450, Hohokam influence prevailed in southern Arizona and northern Mexico. The abandonment of Casa Grande and Pueblo Grande marks the end of the Classic Hohokam. Pima oral history tradition describes how elite Hohokam leaders became oppressive and locals drove them back to the south, as part of a liberation movement. Pima warriors used to sing:

The Gray Spider magician
He made a square Kiaha
He is indeed a magician.
They are shouting, they are shouting,
Around the hill of Atci
The poor people there are shouting
As the news of battle comes.

Canyon de Chelly "Rocky Canyon" National Monument
(Circa 350-1300)

A decade ago, a Hopi woman elder introduced me to Canyon de Chelly. We were standing on the rim, overlooking a breathtaking panorama, when hundreds of swallows suddenly appeared. These little birds, who live communally, fly with lightning speed, zigzagging through the forces of nature. She explained that swallows, like eagles, are messengers carrying people's prayers. They travel spiritually from the Fourth World back to the Third, and from the Middle to the Underworld.

This canyon is known as a place of life and death. In A.D. 306, according to tree ring dating, an underground pithouse was constructed in a place now called Mummy Cave in Canyon del Muerto, the Canyon of the Dead. Beautiful baskets, yucca sandals, and fur blankets were well preserved in the warm, dry atmosphere.

By A.D. 350, people were moving from pithouses to above-ground homes and were skilled basketmakers. Their polychrome coiled burden baskets were conical and were carried using a tumpline strap across the forehead. Some were decorated with lightning and supernatural designs.

After 500, the people of Canyon de Chelly made Tusayan white-and-gray pots. By 850, they were making

▲ *Interior detail, Besh-ba-gowah Pueblo, Globe, Arizona. The Salado site was occupied from A.D. 1225 to 1400.* ▶ *Montezuma Castle, Montezuma Castle National Monument, Arizona. The area was occupied by Hohokam, Hakataya, Sinagua, and Hopi people from about A.D. 600 to 1400.*

Kayenta black-and-white pots and had acquired the architectural knowledge to design pueblo villages: Antelope House, White House, Sliding Rock, and Mummy Cave. They became master stone masons, devoting long hours to inlaying mosaic designs. First Chaco, then Mesa Verde influences took hold. The people lived in relative tranquillity for three centuries and in the third century reaped their greatest agricultural bounty.

From 1150 through two generations, the droughts came. Refugees arrived, one clan after another following the riverbed. At Antelope House, a moiety system formed, with two groups of clans embracing a central plaza. They stayed for nearly 250 years. About 1300, they resumed migration in search of their rightful place. Some resettled at Hopi.

Between 1370 and 1390, the *Asa* Wild Mustard or Tansy Mustard, and their related Warrior Kachina Woman Clan stopped at Canyon de Chelly. They migrated from near Santa Fe, New Mexico, stopping at Santo Domingo, Laguna, Acoma, and Zuni en route to Hopi. They built a village on Antelope Mesa near Awatobi before settling near Walpi. The clans fought side-by-side with their Tewa cousins of Hano to defend Hopiland against the Utes.

Around 1780, during another severe drought, leaders of the Wild Mustard Clan recalled their refreshing stay at Canyon de Chelly and decided to return. They built homes and planted crops, and many intermarried with the Diné Navajo who had moved into the area. The Wild Mustard people moved back to First Mesa at Hopi after the drought, but the Navajo stayed. To this day, Diné families herd sheep, ride horses, and harvest fields of corn, beans, squash, pumpkins, and juicy watermelons in Canyon de Chelly.

One Diné oral history tradition describes how the "Anasazi" of Canyon de Chelly were destroyed by a violent tornado and firestorm. They were said to have delved into taboo areas, the realm of the forbidden.

Petrified Forest National Park
(Circa 6000 B.C.-twentieth century)

Over two hundred twenty-five million years ago, during the Triassic Age, a thick forest of giant trees stood between the plateau of the Anasazi and highlands of the Mogollon. Over time, some trees washed into lowlands where the process of petrification began. Once home to giant reptiles and, later, dinosaurs, it is now a land of fallen giant logs.

Southeast of the Petrified Forest, according to Zuni oral history, there was once a beautiful lake named *Koluwala:wa*. Beneath the lake was the Kachinas' village, where one heard powerful songs and saw spiritual dances.

Every four years, Zuni religious leaders make a pilgrimage to this sacred site to pray and make offerings.

Hanlibinkya, a sandstone canyon east of the Petrified Forest, is covered with Zuni clan markings. This is where Zuni clans were named, according to oral history. Here, where fresh water bubbled down the cliffs, the Zuni twin war gods, the *Ahayuda*, were created by the Sun Father.

The first people in the area date back to 6000 B.C. About a.d. 300, the first settlers arrived. Fresh water nourished the first corn, grown here before A.D. 500. Early farmers built a small village of twenty-five pithouses now called the Flattop site. Their vegetable seeds were a species developed in Mesoamerica, cultivated to acclimate in the Southwest, where rainfall often is less than ten inches per year.

Puerco Ruin, a seventy-five-room pueblo, was built between 1100 and 1400 A.D. Agate House, an eight-room pueblo, was built partially with colorful petrified wood as building blocks. The people who lived at Puerco Ruin may have been star gazers who followed a solar cycle. Their summer solstice marker aligns every year on June 21. In rock art in the Petrified Forest, male and female fertility figures dance under symbols of the Sun, Moon, and Stars.

Evidence of artistic expression in the Petrified Forest is found in the remains of architecture, pottery, basketry, textiles, jewelry, and rock art. More than six hundred ancient sites are preserved within the park.

Homol'ovi Ruins State Park
(Circa 1250-1600)

Since the Archaic era, people have lived along the Little Colorado River, named Paayu by the Hopi. Many travelers on the east-west route favored the river trail winding past Homol'ovi, which means "Place of the Buttes." One village site, Homol'ovi II, is flanked by several buttes. The Homol'ovi area was an excellent location for finding chert, petrified wood, and quartzite to make stone tools, as well as clay for pots and sandstone for construction. The soil was too thin for most vegetables, but good for cotton near the river. In 1896, Jessie Walter Fewkes, archaeologist for the federal Bureau of Ethnology, began excavation of this site.

Adams and Hays excavated Homol'ovi more fully, uncovering sixty-four thousand artifacts plus forty-two thousand sherds. The oldest pottery sherd was Tsegi, from about 600 A.D. More than two-thirds of the sherds were Jeddito yellow-ware, made at Hopi between 1350 and 1400. Pots were traded with Hopi, Zuni, and White Mountain.

From 1256 to 1442, Homol'ovi II, a seven-hundred-room pueblo near Winslow, Arizona, was occupied by ancestors of Hopi and Zuni clans. The people of Homol'ovi traded cotton for Hopi pottery and other goods. Among the artifacts found were corn-grinding stones and a *piki* griddle, used in making Hopi blue corn *piki* bread. Obsidian and red ochre pigment were imported through trade. Other trade goods found around Homol'ovi included sea shells from the

Gulf of California, shell bracelets, and beads from Southern Arizona, as well as turquoise, hematite, and textiles.

The presence of the Kachina Society is evident at Homol'ovi. More than seventy-five Kachina images were painted here as rock art, similar to those found at Hopi. They included Maasaw, Tawa, Giant Ogre, Mudhead, Sio Shalako, Tsakwaina, and some warrior Kachinas. Among them was a pottery fragment with a Sun Forehead Clan Kachina face resembling *Tawa*, the Sun spirit being, with a small, rectangular toothed mouth. Most of the Homol'ovi rock art Kachina masks are round or rectangular with small dot eyes and headgear. Some have bared teeth.

Pottery designs featured ritual and other life forms. Potters discovered new symbols. Clans gathered around Homol'ovi, bringing new cultural influences. Homol'ovi became a staging area to prepare for acceptance at Hopi.

According to Hopi tradition, the Palatkwabi clans settled here before entering Hopi. Palatkwabi was far to the south, where the Water, Sand, Tobacco, and other clans started their northern migrations. The Water people eventually resettled at Walpi and on Second Mesa.

In 1632, Homol'ovi and some Little Colorado settlements were still occupied, but constant Apache raids threatened the people and disrupted trade. By 1650, Homol'ovi was abandoned. The survivors moved to Hopi, Zuni, and other pueblos.

Montezuma Castle National Monument
(Circa 600-1400)

The fertile Verde Valley, where Montezuma Castle and Tuzigoot National Monuments are today, was formed when ancient lakes drained. It became an ideal homeland for animals and later for people.

Natural limestone alcoves and salt deposits that were only a few miles away attracted the ancient ancestors of Puebloan peoples to the area of Montezuma Castle. Seven miles away, Montezuma's Well, producing an amazing one thousand gallons of water per minute, attracted numerous wild animals, thus assuring good hunting. Hohokam canal builders cut channels to irrigate crops.

Ancient peoples constructed their homes of limestone chunks and used local basalt to make grinding stones and stone axes. Obsidian was used for arrowheads, spear points, and knives. Soft clay was formed into pottery bowls. Body paints were produced from mineral deposits: iron oxide for red, malachite for green, azurite for blue and volcanic ash for white. Calcite crystals and red claystone were used for jewelry and ritual objects.

Salt was mined for trade. Once, a tunnel dug deep into the salt deposits collapsed, burying ancient miners alive. Their mummified bodies were later found—victims of one of America's oldest mining disasters.

Trade goods from Mesoamerica came up a route that connected Montezuma's Castle in the Verde Valley to the Hopi Mesas via Homol'ovi, Chavez Pass, and Stoneman Lake. The trail was traveled most heavily during the fourteenth century. Trade slowed to a crawl after political collapse in the south and the arrival of Europeans.

Tuzigoot "Crooked Water" National Monument
(Circa 1000-1450)

Tuzigoot is situated high on a hilltop overlooking the Verde River, a site created by wind and water erosion. Fertile soil for planting crops was left behind when the river changed course, leaving a marshy depression.

Hohokam clans, closely related to southern peoples at Montezuma's Castle, lived in the area before Tuzigoot was built, but most of the construction is Sinagua style. From their village high on a ridge, they could see movements of people and animals across the Verde River Valley. Around 1125, northerners came from Sinagua territory. The Sinagua were mostly farmers who had overpopulated lands around Sunset Crater volcano and migrated in search of more fertile land. Some were accepted at Tuzigoot, while others went on to Montezuma's Castle.

Pot sherds of the Kayenta Anasazi style have been found at Tuzigoot, although there no other evidence of these ancient peoples has been discovered. The pottery probably arrived through trade, rather than because the Kayenta themselves lived there.

Tuzigoot people—multilingual, strategically located, and with family ties to three cultures—became natural traders. They offered minerals, salt, and cotton and were middlemen in the shell-bead and parrot-feather trade. Although they may have tapped into the fortune in silver, zinc, and copper that was buried undertround, no direct evidence has been discovered that they did so.

Walnut Canyon National Monument
(Circa 1050-1275)

About ten miles north of Walnut Canyon stand the San Francisco Peaks, the Mountains of the Kachinas. They are the traditional home of the Hopi Kachinas. The powerful Kachina Clan may have come originally from Muiobi, along the Rio Grande in New Mexico.

The Badger Clan was also believed to come from those mountains, from a spring called Kisiu-va. Their medicine people were powerful and famous healers.

In 1064, when Sunset Crater volcano erupted fifteen miles to the north, Walnut Canyon became a place of refuge for the Badger Clan. They climbed up the steep cliffs of the canyon, snuggled in under the limestone overhangs, and began sealing up the outside of their shelters with stone and clay. They constructed about four hundred small rooms.

Here they stayed for two centuries, eking out a marginal existence. They hunted deer, although carrying a carcass up the steep cliffs must have been a dangerous undertaking.

They found wild berries, piñon, and other natural foods. The surrounding forest was thick with fir, juniper, and aspen. The canyon is named for wild black walnut trees.

Farming was a challenge on the small canyon rim plots, where the farmers had to climb to the top. In the mid-thirteenth century the dry years came, and their luck ran out. By 1275, the last family packed up and left. The Badger Clan eventually resettled at Tuwanacabi, north of the Hopi villages. They built a new village not far from Oraibi, called Siu-va, named after a nearby spring.

A decade ago, I made friends with the late John Lansa, a Hopi Badger Clan elder from Old Oraibi, who possessed a remarkable ability to find ancient sites from oral history traditions. Once, he slept on my couch at night while searching daily for the shrine farthest west. He found it!

Just before passing into the next world at almost one hundred years old, John scribbled a note to me with the little stub pencil he kept in his shirt pocket:

> Well, I'm almost blind now, and I can't hear much anymore. But I'm still standing up for my rights and praying for the whole world. I can't wait 'til next spring, so I can plant my fields. Keep up the good work, Greg.
> Your Friend,
> Lansa

Wupatki "Tall House" National Monument, Sunset Crater (Circa 9000-6000 B.C., 5000-2000 B.C., 500-675, 675-1064, 1075-1225)

Wupatki National Monument embraces 35,254 acres between Flagstaff and the Hopi mesas. Archaeologists have surveyed and inventoried over twenty-seven hundred sites where ancient people of at least a dozen different groups lived, hunted, farmed, and built homes. The oldest artifact is an eleven-thousand-year-old Clovis spearpoint used to hunt mammoth elephants. Over the next ten millennia, groups of people walked through, sometimes building pithouses and living for several generations before moving on.

On July 5, 1054, a star exploded at the tip of a crescent Moon—a supernova called Crab Nebula. During the next decade, a series of earthquakes further alerted Hopi Bear Clan chiefs and their assemblies of spiritual leaders at Shungopavi and Oraibi. A ten-mile-long crack opened in Mother Earth.

In the autumn of 1064, from high atop the Hopi mesas, a smoky cloud could be seen on the southwestern horizon toward Nuvatikyao, the Snow Peaks now called the San Francisco Mountains. Sunset Crater volcano, sixty miles away, was on the verge of a major eruption. Hopi tradition recorded:

> They all at once noticed a light in the San Francisco Mountains . . . The next night. . .the fire in the mountains appeared to be larger . . . and larger . . . During the fourth night the people again continued their gambling and carousing . . . those outside watching with great alarm.

A Hopi spiritual interpretation suggests that *Yaponcha*, the Wind Spirit, may have been angered by people's failure to remember that the Third World was destroyed by gambling and corruption. *Yaponcha* spewed from the Underworld as molten lava and streamed five miles down the mountainside, destroying everything in its fiery path. Volcanic ash rained across the valley and beyond the Hopi mesas, falling more than a foot deep on nearby homes. An estimated half billion tons of cinders blanketed an eight-hundred-square-mile area, with smoke drifting all the way to Kansas.

Repeating a tradition that would continue for a millennium, Hopi priests journeyed toward the mountains, leaving offerings in pottery bowls at the Ice Caves. The breath of *Yaponcha*, now cold and crisp, can be felt to this day, blowing from deep underground through cracks in black, frozen lava beds.

Two years later, in 1066, the volcano erupted again as Haley's Comet streaked across the sky. Fires from the upper and lower worlds must have made a powerful impression on ancient priests, who connected ceremonial cycles with solar, lunar, and cosmic cycles. They were anxious to restore peace and harmony on Earth.

In 1120, Wupatki Pueblo was founded by the Bear Clan, according to the Hopi:

> The Bear Clan stopped . . . [at] Wupatki . . . After a while the wise old men told the Bear Clan people, "This is not the place we are supposed to go to . . . Let us move on. Our guiding spirit will take care of us."

Other Puebloan farmers—Sinagua, Kayenta from the north, and perhaps Salt-Gila River Hohokam from the south—discovered that volcanic ash created mulch that retained moisture, promoting growth of vegetation. Bountiful rains and this discovery caused what has been described as a "prehistoric land rush." Thousands migrated to the area. Increased population caused rapid soil depletion, which may explain the large number of sites.

Farmers planted vegetable gardens and fields of Hopi cotton. The cotton was used to weave beautiful textiles, breechcloths for daily wear, and robes for ceremonial use. Their finest fabrics have fifty-three warps and fifty-three wefts per inch in plain tapestry weave. They also blended plain weaves with diagonal two-by-two twill, in designs that look like crashing waves and lightning bolts. Cloth has been found that was tie-dyed—the technique popular among the Hippies of the 1960s. Rare miniature twill blankets, probably shrine offerings, were discovered at Wupatki, Keet Seel, and Bat Cave, and at a Jemez shrine in New Mexico.

By 1212, construction was completed at Wupatki and other local, multicultural pueblos. The "Tall House" community was three stories high. More than one hundred rooms have now been rebuilt. Park Service surveys inside the monument have identified twenty-six hundred pueblos and have found volcanic faultlines—called earthcracks—crisscrossing the area.

The Salt-River Hohokam visited and spread their Mesoamerican-influenced ideologies, sports, art, and architecture within the area. In 1150, a Southern-style ball court was built at Wupatki.

In 1212, the last log was cut and placed into Wupatki Pueblo. Construction was underway on the nearby Lomaki Beautiful House, Citadel, Nalakihu, and Wukoko Big House Pueblos.

A generation later, over-population resulted in overworking the soil. By 1225, families were leaving. According to Hopi tradition, most moved to Homol'ovi before finally setting at Hopi and other Southwest pueblos.

Navajo National Monument: Betatakin "Ledge House" and Keet Seel "Broken Pottery" (Circa 950-1300)

Classic cliff dwellings, Betatakin and Keet Seel, were homes for certain clans, according to respected Hopi elders. Their ancestors were said to be spiritual people responsible for maintaining powerful religious ceremonies. Over a century ago, federal archaeologist Jessie Walter Fewkes recorded their oral history traditions:

"The ancient home of my ancestors," said a Snake chief to Fewkes in the 1890s, "was called Tokonabi [Betatakin], which is situated not far from Navaho Mountain. If you go there, you will find ruins of their former houses."

While Betatakin was the Snake Clan village, Keet Seel was the Horn Clan village. Together with the Flute people and others, these clans brought important ceremonies to Hopi. Here we find the origins of the Snake Dance, a sacred ceremony in which priests dance with live rattlesnakes in their mouths—and, incredibly, are not bitten. The purpose of the ceremony is to deliver prayers for the benefit of the whole world.

In the late nineteenth century, archaeologist Victor Mindeleff interviewed Hopi Horn and Flute Clan people. They described the land from they had come:

The Horn people, to which the Lenbaki [Flute] belonged, have a legend of coming from a mountain range in the east . . . Its peaks were always snow covered, and the trees were always green. From the hillside, the plains were seen, over which roamed the deer, the antelope, and the bison, feeding on never-failing grasses . . . twining through these plains were streams of bright water, beautiful to look upon, a place where none but those who were of our people ever gained access.

The clan elders described their cliff-dwellings at Betatakin and Keet Seel:

[At] a canyon with high, steep walls, in which was a flowing stream . . . they built a large house in the cavernous recess, high up in the canyon wall. They tell of devoting two years to ladder making and cutting and pecking shallow holes up the steep rocky side by which to mount to the cavern, and three years more were employed in building the house . . .

Snake and Horn Clan elders recounted the lives of their ancestors at Betatakin and Keet Seel. One day, a stranger ventured into their territory. The man, who was Hopi, described his beloved homeland in the South. Some Horn Clan men agreed to follow him to see this beautiful place, Hopiland:

After some stay he left and was accompanied by a party of the "Horn" [clan], who were to visit the land occupied by their kindred Hopituh and return with an account of them; but they never came back. After waiting a long time another band was sent, who returned and said that the first emissaries had found wives and had built houses on the brink of a beautiful canyon, not far from the other Hopituh dwellings. After this many of the Horns grew dissatisfied with their cavern home, dissensions arose, they left their home and finally they reached Tusayan [Hopiland].

Other Hopi clans hold oral history traditions of coming with the Snake and Horn people from Betatakin and Keet Seel. These clans originally resettled near First Mesa.

Betatakin was a 135-room village, built of sandstone, inside a huge cave. The cave measures 450 feet high and 370 feet wide. A natural spring still nourishes groves of trees, a cool place of refuge in the midst of a harsh environment. Construction began in 1269, and the last log was cut in 1286, according to tree ring dating.

Keet Seel is one of the largest and best-preserved cliff dwellings in Arizona. Three centuries older than Betatakin, Keet Seel was inhabited by 950, but was redesigned starting in 1272. The final structure featured 160 rooms and a 180-foot-wall built by master stone masons. By 1300, the Horn Clan people and the Betatakin Snake Clan people left for Hopiland.

▲ *Lomaki Ruin, Box Canyon, Wupatki National Monument, Arizona, was home to Sinagua, Mogollan, and Hisatsinomcirca A.D. 1075 to 1225.* ▶ *Tsegi Canyon, Canyon de Chelly National Monument, Arizona, once home to Pueblo Badger, Butterfly, and Wild Mustard Clans, is now Diné Navajo land.*

Ancient Peoples of Utah

Hovenweep "Deserted Canyon" National Monument
(Circa 500-1290)

Hovenweep is most famous for its majestic stone towers. Described as castles by nineteenth-century explorers, they appear like a mirage, the setting for some medieval fairy tale. These imposing structures, every stone painstakingly hand-shaped, were raised in the desert to provide high vantage points for people to observe distant horizons and the heavens beyond. Hovenweep may have been the home of ancient astronomers.

People roamed this desert area long before the castles were built. Around 12,000 B.C., big game hunters tracked mammoth elephants through Deserted Canyon, thirty-five miles west of Mesa Verde. Paleolithic groups hunted deer, elk, antelope, and rabbit for food, leather, and furs.

Hunters poised with spear throwers, called *atlatls*, are painted on rock walls. Similar images can be found from Mexico to Texas and California.

Around A.D. 500, Mesa Verde families settled in the Hovenweep area. They constructed their villages on the mesa ridges and surrounding flatlands. Good, rich soil along the San Juan River produced bountiful crops of corn, beans, squash, watermelons, and other Mesoamerican vegetables. The natural springs nearby were channeled to irrigate terraced vegetable gardens with seeps through an ingenious network of reservoirs and canals. The waters nurtured a variety of native herbs and plants including bee-weed, ground cherry, milkweed, cattail, wolf berry, and sedge grasses.

By 750, the population had tripled, and clusters of pithouse villages had been constructed. By 900, neighbors had moved into nearby locations, including Edge of the Cedars, Lowry, and Three Kiva to the north. Slow growth continued for centuries.

The influence of the Chaco, Mesa Verde, and Aztec cultures soon reached Hovenweep, with the rate of change accelerating around 1150. Architects and engineers constructed larger pueblos with stone towers at the head of box canyons.

Master masons set to work on masterpieces in classic Mesa Verde style. Their towers were more than feats of engineering; evidence is mounting that the structures were astronomical observatories. Hopi and other Puebloan priests still track the path of the sun through the tops of kivas, from notches carved into portals to align with Tawa, the sun, and Pliades, Orion, and other constellations. Hovenweep towers constructed in four shapes—circles, ovals, squares, and half circles—were found in Chacoan city plans. Peepholes atop the towers provided vantage points for observing things that were important to the well-being of Hovenweep.

Hovenweep's "Sun Room" is attached to a half-circle tower. Peepholes align at summer and winter solstices and at spring and fall equinoxes. At these four annual solar events, sunlight streams through the portals directed at key markers on the wooden beam atop the doorway. This creates a kind of calendar based on light and shadow. By precisely marking these dates, the priests could plan their ceremonial cycles in harmony with the social and agricultural seasons.

The music of rattles and drums faded as the people of Hovenweep moved away around 1300.

Edge of the Cedars State Park
(Circa 800-950, 1025-1125, 1200-1300)

Resting atop a ridge with a panoramic view, Edge of the Cedars Pueblo stood in the center of a triangle formed by the Delores, San Juan, and Colorado Rivers. Mesoamerican vegetables grew in the gardens. Hunters stalked antelope in the valley and deer in the foothills of the Abuja, the Blue Mountains. From this vantage point, Shiprock rises on the southeast horizon, a prominent landmark for ancient peoples for over ten thousand years.

About twelve hundred years ago, Northern San Juan people began building Pueblo-style homes above ground out of clay and sticks. More complex stone structures were constructed as the villages were expanded from Mesa Verde to the Montezuma Valley and east of Blanding on Alkali Ridge.

By the eleventh century, this community may have included six groups of clans, since the city plan expanded to accommodate six residential complexes. The community layout may reflect successive settlements. The religious societies were organized around ten kivas, plus one Great Kiva for united functions. Today, climbing down the ladder into the sole restored kiva, one experiences an intimate rectangular ceremonial space similar to those that are still active at Hopi.

Northern San Juan people were master artists and crafts people. Their skillful basketmakers used willow and yucca to produce beautiful bowls, trays, and other forms. They warmed themselves with rabbit fur and turkey feather blankets. An abundance of deer provided meat and leather. They designed their pottery with balanced patterns. Archeologists have found a special stone room which was

---

◄ *Hovenweep Castle at Hovenweep National Monument, Utah, was occupied by the San Juan and Mesa Verde Anasazi from about* A.D. *1150 to 1290.*

their "tool shed," a storage place for bone awls, stone hoes, and flint knives.

That trade routes from Mexico reached Edge of the Cedars is evidenced by an ancient copper bell and other artifacts that have been found at the site. Colorful macaw and parrot feather regalia, as well as turkey feather capes, are preserved today in a professionally curated museum on the site. Stored in this facility are rows of beautiful pottery and thousands of bags of artifacts. Among their best-kept secrets are giant stone phallic sculptures, one almost three feet long and a foot wide, weighing well over a hundred pounds.

Fertility and the perpetuation of life were a paramount concern and the focus of important spiritual societies. The concept of love as a sacred act has ancient roots.

Mule Canyon, Cedar Mesa Area
(Circa 750-1300)

For two and one-half centuries, Mule Canyon was a small satellite community. Then life changed dramatically about the year 1000. Two culture groups arrived, the Kayenta from the south and the Mesa Verde people from the west. Both groups brought their own unique cultural traditions, pottery, architecture, and world views. Engineers built a small dam.

The tall stone tower at Mule Canyon is just one in a network of towers with sequential visual contact across this entire area. These towers may have served as "web sites" in an "Anasazi Internet."

Evidence indicates that a communication language may have been developed using mica mirrors, crystal reflectors, or smoke signals. Mirrors and reflectors have been found at the sites.

When the message was received, the lookout would have walked through a secret tunnel into an underground kiva where traditional leaders gathered. A second tunnel led to a double-wing complex where the news would have been delivered. The theory of inter-tower communication has been advanced by scholars at the respected School of American Research.

The masonry in the main kiva at Mule Canyon is masterful. The fire pit is designed with a stone deflector and ventilator shaft. A niche built into the wall could have supported religious altars. These concepts are harmonious with Hopi styles, while the circular plan is a feature of Rio Grande Pueblo kivas.

Underground tunnels and secret passageways are important for ritual dramas enacted during ceremonies. These rituals still are practiced at Hopi and other pueblos. Out of respect, many details are kept secret. Elders explain that one must be prepared mentally, physically, and emotionally to be initiated into these spiritual societies. One elder said, "The uninitiated might go crazy, mentally ill, if they learned these things improperly." It is enough to say that some of the horrors that destroyed previous worlds have come back to life.

Natural Bridges National Monument
(Circa 1-1300)

More than two hundred ancient sites exist within this seven-thousand-acre preserve, featuring dramatic geologic formations that have been created by the forces of nature. The Natural Bridges, three monumental sandstone arches formed by wind and water erosion, are named in Hopi *Sipapu*, *Kachina*, and *Owachomo*. *Sipapu* is thought to be the Earth's navel. *Kachina* is a spirit being. *Owachomo* may refer to an old type of Coal Kachina.

From the traditional Puebloan perspective, the Natural Bridges take on legendary and supernatural proportions. The forces of wind and water that created these landmarks are powerful beings in Pueblo spirituality. Migration paths trace the Puebloan search for the Middle Place, the center of the universe.

Six directions and sky colors radiate from the center of the Tewa world. They are North, blue-green; West, yellow; South, red; East, white; Above, all colors; and Below, black. Spiritual beings, sacred mountains and religious shrines exist in each direction, spiraling in toward the center. Directional energies flow through the power of wind and rain water delivered from storm systems, spiraling outward from the center. Upon death, according to Hopi beliefs, one may become a "Kachina in the clouds."

The sound of the wind is created in Pueblo ceremonies by an oval wooden slat with a long string called a bullroar, or *watu* in the Tewa language. The most powerful Tewa wind deity is an elder female spirit called *Wakwijo*. In the

▲ *Lightning strikes at Hovenweep Castle, Hovenweep National Monument, Utah. Through lightning and rain, Father Sky touches Mother Earth, the cosmic "love affair."* ▶ *Handprints adorn Ancient Indian Ruin at Cedar Mesa, Utah. Pure pigment was blown through bone tubes to imprint hand "signatures."*

Hopi Powamu purification ceremony, powerful Kachinas whirl bullroars over their heads. Their deep, vibratory sounds are eerie. The bullroar made for the author has a rainbow painted on one side, and tadpoles on the other. Tadpoles grow to bull frogs, whose calls are replicated with a gourd rasp in ceremonies intended to attract rain—gentle, nourishing rains, not violent, destructive storms. The environmental forces that created the Natural Bridges are the same forces Pueblo people seek to attract in their rain-making ceremonies.

Rock art in this area displays a pantheon of supernatural beings and ceremonial figures, many wearing headdresses with one or two horns. Many of the figures appear to be associated with the Kwan One Horn Society and the A'alt Two Horn Society. Hopi societal leaders explain that One and Two Horns are "protectors of all land and life," and the "protectors of the inner circle around the ceremonies." One center of the Horn Clan was located less than one hundred miles south of Natural Bridges at Tokonabi [Navajo] Mountain. Hopi Clan symbols have been identified around Natural Bridges.

Grand Gulch Primitive Area
(Circa 200-1300)

Early archaeologist Richard Wetherill, of Mesa Verde fame, found that Grand Gulch was an important location of the pre–Cliff Dweller culture. Known as "Basketmakers," these people are characteristic of the earliest-known phase of "Anasazi" settlement in the Southwest. Before the invention of pottery, they wove beautiful coiled, twined and plaited baskets. Inside a cave, Wetherill discovered a thousand years of layered debris, and at the bottom were ancient baskets.

The American Museum of Natural History and the Heye Foundation's Museum of the American Indian divided Wetherill's Grand Gulch basket collection. The latter half now is in the new National Museum of the American Indian. The weavings exemplify great diversity in fiber art techniques, materials, and design. Polychrome coiled baskets demonstrate the makers' skills in dying materials red, black, and other colors. Some have single-rod foundations, similar to Paiute and Washo baskets. Others are two-rod with bundle foundations, unlike contemporary basketry construction. The plaited sifter baskets used in winnowing natural grains are woven of yucca in an over-two-under-two weave. Once, this author took pictures of Mesa Verde baskets to a master Hopi weaver, and she duplicated the designs with ease. Today, the baskets she made are part of an educational collection.

Archaic rock art found in sandstone rock shelters at Grand Gulch includes abstract, multi-colored designs of

◄ *An ancient Indian ruin, southeast Utah. This area was occupied from about* A.D. *1150 to 1300.*

zigzag snakes or lightning, water waves, and ghostly circles with tails. Similar paintings throughout the Great Basin demonstrate parallels among ancient Southwest people. Perhaps the most intimate pictograph at Grand Gulch is of a woman giving birth to a baby.

Evidence of the presence of Green Masked Kachinas has been found both in rock art and in the form of an ancient headdress. A Hopi Singer Society elder once explained that the color green symbolizes "all the green growing things." The singers are prophets who sing their visions of the future.

Anasazi Indian Village State Park or Coombs Site
(Circa 1075-1275)

For two centuries, Kayenta people prospered on the Aquarious Plateau. This village was small, less than two hundred people. The layout indicates two main clusters of homes, perhaps representing two clans or a moiety structure. However, several kivas supported a complex of spiritual societies. The location of the village, in what is now southern Utah, placed it at a cultural crossroads. During the time it was occupied, Pueblo Bonito was under construction and Chaco exerted wide influence. Hohokam traders ventured up southern trails. Lowry Pueblo, Farview near Mesa Verde, and Yellow Jacket in Montezuma Valley were the three major trade centers for outlying villages.

The most unique feature of the pueblo at Anasazi State Park is how it met its demise. Fire destroyed the pueblo; how the fire started remains a mystery. When the Hopi village of Awatovi, near First Mesa, became corrupt and evil, a decision was made to destroy it by fire. According to Hopi oral history, pine sap or piñon pitch was smeared onto the walls and the place was set ablaze.

Newspaper Rock and Canyonlands National Park
(Circa 7000 B.C. to A.D. 1300)

Can we read the stories on Newspaper Rock? Scholars are now working with Indian descendants to decipher the symbols. Elders recite traditions related to these ancient writings and pictures. Like linguists wrestling with Egyptian hieroglyphics or the Mayan Codices, archeo-cryptologists are exploring original sources to crack the code.

Newspaper Rock is a four-thousand-year-old "bulletin board" where generations of artists have painted over and over on the same space. Numerous clan symbols appear— Snake, Horn, Deer, Bear, Crane—as well as bighorn sheep. There is even a later addition of an Indian hunter shooting an arrow at an elk. Using computers, scholars may be able to lift the layers of images by time periods without touching the surface of the rock. This would allow us to see the designs era-by-era.

A few miles to the west is Canyonlands National Park, an area similar to the Grand Canyon. The "Great Gallery" in the Horseshoe Canyon Maze area presents ancient and masterful examples of monumental spirit beings that resemble rare depictions of the Creator on an important Hopi Bear Clan Tablet. The images were created with a variety of techniques, including the use of fine yucca brushes and reed tubes to blow pigments onto smooth sandstone walls. Textural shading was added by carving patterns into colored areas, a technique called intaglio by Michelangelo and other Italian Renaissance artists.

Fremont Indian State Park
(Circa 875-1250)

North of Bryce Canyon and west of Canyonlands is Fremont Indian State Park. Fremont culture was made up of the northern relations of Kayenta intermixed with peoples of the Great Basin. In this area, ancient ancestors of the Hopi northern clans, along with Shoshones, Paiutes and Utes, spoke Uto-Aztecan languages. They influenced the Athabaskan ancestors of the Diné Navajo and Apaches who migrated in small groups from the Northwest. The Fremont people are considered an integration of these cultural sources.

Three major cultural and environmental areas intersect in central Utah—Great Basin, Pueblo, and Plains. The surrounding Sevier Fremont villages are known today as Grantsville, Tooele, Hinckley Farm, Nephi, Pharo Village, Ephraim, Backhoe Village, Snake Rock Village, Old Woman, and Popular Knob. There are ten times as many temporary camps as villages in the area.

From Desert Archaic roots, these people began as big game hunters who also collected wild herbs and natural grains. They later accepted Mesoamerican vegetables and planted gardens.

Their pottery was Pueblo-influenced and known as Ivie Creek Black-on-White, Snake Valley Black-on-Gray and Sevier Gray. Their architecture, which began as Archaic pithouses, later reflected the technology of the south. They wore Plains-style hide moccasins, wove single rod baskets like the Paiute, and carved incised tablets like the Hopi.

Their artists also fired clay figurines similar in appearance to the Tesuque Rain Gods, with almond eyes, long noses, earrings, and elaborate necklaces with rows of oval pendants. Similar figures appear in Fremont rock art. Their masterfully shaped bone rings, tools, and tubes are unique. Through bone tubes, artists blew pigments on rock art, and healers sucked dark forces out of their patients in ritual curing ceremonies.

Three Kiva Pueblo
(Circa 900-1300)

The sound of turkeys gobbling once filled the air in the area around Three Kiva Pueblo. The native birds were raised in a two-by-twenty-foot turkey run that still exists in its weathered condition. Turkey bone whistles were blown to the heavens by spiritual leaders who wore turkey feather capes. Abalone pendants from the Pacific Ocean and trade goods from Mesoamerica show that this community was connected with distant places.

Around 900, a fourteen-room village was constructed, the first of three periods of occupation. Kayenta from northeast Arizona founded the pueblo. They may have been related to the Horn and Snake Clans from Betatakin and Keet Seel near Navajo Mountain. They maintained important religious ceremonies, including the Snake Dance, which they later carried to Hopi.

The people built three kivas, the underground religious chambers for which the pueblo was named. The three kivas may indicate the presence of three spiritual societies, possibly related to the Snake, Horn, and Flute Clans. These Tokonabi people belonged to the Snake, Antelope, One Horn, Two Horn, Blue Flute, Grey Flute, and other religious organizations.

After A.D. 1000, influence from the west arrived, as the Mesa Verde and Hovenweep communities grew and spread their influence. Three Kiva Pueblo was expanded into a square with a central plaza. There in the center of the pueblo, spiritual societies emerged from the kivas to perform their ceremonies before the people of the village. Deep-voiced chants, drumbeats, rattles, and the melodic sound of flutes were composed to help bring the people of the village into harmony with the higher forces of the cosmos.

One of the kivas has been reconstructed, making it is possible to cimb down its ladder and gain a sense of the ancient ancestors of the past.

▲ An ancient Indian ruin still boasts its original stucco, painting, and pictograph. This ruin dates from about A.D. 1150 to 1300. ▶ Sunset and moonrise combine over Holly Castle, in Hovenweep National Monument, Utah. The Hovenweep area was occupied from about A.D. 1150 to 1290.

Ancient Peoples of New Mexico

Chaco Canyon National Park

Evidence indicates that big game hunters roamed in Chaco Canyon as early as 7000 B.C. They stalked deer, mammoth, bison, antelope, and elk using spear throwers called *atlatls*. Today, their Pueblo descendants are initiated into hunting societies where they conduct ceremonies, carve animal fetishes, and sing sacred songs. With great respect, Zuni hunters prepare for the hunt:

> *I have made ready of the sacred things of my fathers, the priest gods of the sacred dances, the priest gods of the Prey (beings) . . . I shall go forth from here prayerfully upon the trails of my earth-mother.*

Nourished by the natural gifts of the Earth, the ancient people migrated through Chaco Canyon in search of their rightful places. In their quest for the Middle Place, the Zuni stopped for a time at Chaco Canyon, Heshoda Bitsulliya. The Zuni were joined by the Big Fire and Sword Swallower Societies, led by the Bow Priests "sweeping danger out of the way." Chaco Canyon became recognized as a spiritual center that attracted people from far and wide.

About three thousand years ago, people from these migrating clans had become farmers and were living in pithouse settlements at Chaco Canyon. For centuries, they grew mostly corn and squash. Then, around 600 B.C., beans were introduced from Mesoamerica, where the Olmec culture was flourishing. The three vegetables, grown together, improved their diet. There was, as yet, no pottery, but the women of that period wove beautiful baskets.

About A.D. 500, life changed for the Chaco people at settlements such as Shabik'eshchee village. Bows and arrows were developed, as were spindle whorls for spinning the cotton which had just been introduced. Ancient ancestors of the San Juan, Santa Clara, San Ildefonso, Nambe, Tesuque, and Pojoaque peoples left the main Tanoan group and gradually developed the Tewa dialect. Tewa descendants assert that some of their ancestors lived at Chaco.

By 650, better building techniques were introduced, called "Anasazi" style. New ideas and trade goods flowed from Mexico. From 850 to 900, Chaco Canyon was transformed from a community of pithouses into a complex of elaborate pueblos designed in circles and half circles. A

◄ Pueblo Bonito, Chaco Culture National Historic Park, New Mexico, was one of the largest pueblos in the Southwest. It was occupied from about A.D. 850 to 1123.

group of master architects from the south inspired Chaco society to work together on a mammoth construction effort. Many pueblos grew to eight hundred rooms and rose five stories high, surrounded by dozens of kivas. The total construction effort required an estimated 215 thousand logs, cut and dragged more than twenty-five miles from the nearest forests.

The structure of Chetro Ketl was built with more than twenty thousand logs. Work on that pueblo began around 900 with "unfaced slab" masonry. A century later, a renovation was completed. According to tree ring dating, the north side was constructed between 1036 and 1040. The upper stories were built between 1043 and 1053.

Wooden spiritual artifacts from Chetro Ketl have many of the same characteristics as those used by Kachina and other spiritual societies today at Hopi, Zuni, and Rio Grande pueblos. A group of Hopi elders identified a lightning lattice among the Chetro Ketl artifacts similar to one still carried by Lightning Man in Powamu, the spring purification ceremony. During this ceremony an eighty-five-year-old elder explained that Lightning Man is warning the world. If we fail to bring the Fourth World back into harmony, he said, Lightning Man will purify the Earth with destructive lightning, winds, floods, and earthquakes. This will mark the dawn of the Fifth World.

Chacoans witnessed the destruction of a world on July 5, 1054, when a brilliant supernova exploded, producing the Crab Nebula. The most intense period of building at Chaco Canyon was from 1055 to 1083. Some clans may have arrived during that period from Sinagua, near Flagstaff.

Pueblo Bonito was built between 1075 and 1123, during a second great construction boom at Chaco Canyon. Over a million hand-shaped, sandstone blocks were carved with stone tools to construct the Great House at Pueblo Bonito. Regional communities, perhaps settled by rival migrating clans, featured new masonry styles. Construction of magnificent multi-storied Great Houses began around 1100.

Chaco became a major trade center. Among the goods exchanged were seashells from the Pacific Ocean and Gulf of Mexico, parrot feathers, and seeds and technologies such as weaving looms from Mexico. More than sixty thousand pieces of jewelry, including turquoise pendants, beads, and precious stone mosaics, have been found at Chaco Canyon.

If Chacoan priests were looking for a sign to further inspire the builders of Pueblo Bonito, the omen arrived on March 7, 1076. A total solar eclipse darkened the daytime sky south of Chaco Canyon. The shadow of the moon cut a large swath across the Southwest. A second solar eclipse occured on July 11, 1097. These astronomical events may have influenced spiritual societies and ceremonies, such as Soyal, based on solar cycles. Solar and lunar cycles are important indicators in Pueblo culture, signaling the time for planting and harvesting crops, as well as other activities. Five astronomical observatories were constructed at Chaco, as well as many more across the Southwest.

In 1130, an even more threatening period began. Rain and snow stopped falling. The soil became alkali encrusted. Animals left. Sources of firewood and logs were depleted. The last log for construction was cut in 1132. Chaco social structure began to wane, and people moved away.

By 1140, the Chacoan outlier system of communities collapsed. Many clans began searching for new homelands. Ancient ancestors of Zia and Santa Ana, Keresan speakers, migrated from Chaco to the Rio Puerco and on to the Rio Grande. Some Taos ancestors moved from Chaco Canyon, as well as from the Chimney Rock-Piedra area east of Durango, Colorado. Tanoans moved from the upper San Juan and Mesa Verde. The drought was described in oral history as a time when "Mother Earth was splitting apart."

Some Zuni Clans migrated from Chaco first to the Jemez Mountains, then to the Sandia Mountains, Mount Taylor, and finally Zuni Pueblo. Uto-Aztecan speakers also tell of of living at Chaco. Some clans from Chaco Canyon and Mesa Verde eventually settled in Hopi. The Sun Clan and others intermarried and spread to Keresan and Tanoan communities. Chacoan influence spread from Hopi in the west to the Rio Grande Valley in the east. From a traditional viewpoint, Chaco was not the center of the universe. People continued their quest for the Middle Place.

Aztec Ruins National Monument
(Circa 1100-1200 and 1125-1300)

In 1106, the first log was cut to build a classic Chacoan-style pueblo at Aztec, a satellite community for regional trade and cultural exchange. It was located fifty miles north of Chaco Canyon, and a well-engineered road began at Chaco and pointed toward Aztec. The road's purpose may have been more spiritual than economic, since shrines were built along the way to Pueblo Bonito and Chetro Ketl.

The 161-thousand-square-foot Great House, built by master Chacoan architects, contained some 450 rooms and was three to five rooms deep and up to three stories high. Over the centuries, rooms were used for various purposes. A round Great Kiva, fifty feet in diameter, was raised in the center of the plaza. Four stout columns, set on 375-pound, hand-carved limestone bases, supported a ninety-five-ton roof. This center of spiritual, social, and political life was a microcosm of the four worlds in the Puebloan cosmos.

Many other kivas were constructed, which may reflect a complex religious structure of spiritual societies. A small kiva was built near the Great Kiva for the maintenance of ceremonies. Some kivas were tri-walled, the inner room within three concentric walls. Some of today's Hopi elders say the "T" shaped kiva doorways symbolize the "window through which we view the world, like traditional Hopi-style haircuts."

By 1125, construction of the major parts of the pueblo had been completed. It contained homes that were cool in summer and warm in winter, their ceilings insulated atop interior beams. Those logs have helped scientists in precise tree-ring dating.

Some scholars say that Northern Aztec styles of architecture, pottery and, perhaps, spirituality, strongly influenced Chaco. Aztec ideologies may have contributed to a shift in administrative and spiritual leadership from Chaco to Aztec. Aztec intellectual achievements are reflected in a sophisticated material culture. They made refined pottery and finely woven baskets with intricate designs. One of the largest caches of turquoise was discovered here.

Aztec farmers diverted water from the Animus River to irrigate fields of corn, beans, squash, and other foods. They may have sent surplus crops to help feed those in Chaco Canyon. The Aztecs grew cotton and were master weavers. They wove diamond and diagonal twill blankets, breech cloths, and sashes and made robes of cotton and rabbit fur.

By 1150, the Chaco complex had collapsed, and some people may have settled temporarily with their cousins at Aztec. But Aztec could have been a temporary shelter at best. It was soon abandoned also. Bad weather may not have been the only problem. Newcomers at other pueblos caused feuds over issues from jealousies to new spiritual inspirations. For whatever reason, residents of Aztec left their pueblo and all their hard work behind and resumed migration, perhaps ultimately settling at Hopi, Zuni, Tanoan, and Keresan-speaking Rio Grande pueblos. The site was again occupied for a time during the 1200s.

Pecos National Historical Park
(Circa 850-1838)

Perched seven thousand feet high in the Sangre de Cristo Mountains, eighteen miles southeast of Santa Fe,

▲ Casa Rinconada, Chaco Culture National Historic Park, New Mexico, was a Great Kiva, accommodating hundreds of people, circa A.D. 1000 to 1200. ▶ A reconstructed Great Kiva at West Ruin, Aztec Ruins National Monument, New Mexico, was a center of spiritual, social, and political life.

Pecos Pueblo sits on a mesa near the Pecos River. Pecos people called their pueblo Kakora, the "Place Down Where the Stone is on Top" and themselves *Pe-Kush,* meaning the "People," in their Towa dialect of the Tanoan language.

Traditional Pecos religious structure was supported by up to sixteen kivas, all facing eastward toward the rising sun, as well as at least two shrines and a sacred cave. Inside one of the kivas, a holy fire was kept burning before a small altar. Spiritual leaders prayed inside these kivas, smoking hand-carved clay pipes with fantastic spirit-being designs.

The Towa (Jemez and Pecos) emerged from the Earth at Wavinatita, a lagoon near Stone Lake in northern New Mexico, south of Dulce. Around 500 B.C., ancient ancestors of the Jemez and Pecos left the main Tanoan group and, in time, developed the Towa dialect. They probably were the so-called Rosa Phase people of the Governador area. By A.D. 1, they were still living near Stone Lake. The Pe-Kush remained in northern New Mexico for many centuries.

Some Towa ancestors of the Jemez and Pecos lived in settlements near Gallina. They constructed monumental cylindrical towers with portals aligned to celestial cycles. Their society was divided into moieties, called Squash and Turquoise, who exchanged power in summer and winter. Some clans moved to Jemez Canyon; others to Galisteo. This may indicate the beginning of the Towa division into Jemez and Pecos peoples. Evidence of division is in the floor plan and construction methods at Unshagi.

Shortly after 1100, the first of three groups of people migrated from the north and settled in the upper Pecos Valley. Towa-speaking ancestors of the Jemez and Pecos peoples moved out of the Gallina area and established villages in the Western Province (San Diego-Virgin Canyon) and Eastern Province (Polica-Vallecitos). Keresan-speaking ancestors of the Zia also lived in the Vallecitos area. After the second group arrived from the west in 1200, they built adobe homes with rare rear doorways adjacent to the kivas.

Towa ancestors settled in the mountains and on the mesas around Jemez, west of Santa Fe. Other Towas settled in Pecos and the Galisteo region south of Santa Fe, extending to Glorieta and Pecos. After 1300, a third group came from the south and built detached circular kivas and homes on the mesa top at Pecos. A century later, the multi-storied pueblo grew around a central plaza.

The Pe-Kush created beautiful spiritual artwork, often depicting the water serpent *Avanyu.* This creature was said to know Mother Earth most intimately, because he lived within her bosom, in deep underground rivers. Perhaps *Avanyu* was related to the parrot headdressed serpent of the Aztec's *Quetzalcoatl. Avanyu* symbols spread throughout the Southwest, down the Rio Grande and among the Hohokam Water Clans in Arizona.

◄ *A ladder leads to an enlarged natural cave at Bandelier National Monument, New Mexico. This area was occupied from about A.D. 1200 to 1590.*

The pottery of these Southwest clans reflects diverse clan traditions—red, black, plain, and polychrome glazed ware. They wore turquoise jewelry and fine clothing made of cotton, feathers, antelope, and buffalo leather and made buffalo hides into headdresses and painted shields.

During the sixteenth century, Spanish conquistadors Francisco Vásquez de Coronado, Antonio de Espejo, and Gaspar Castaño de Sosa stopped at Pecos. In 1598 the first New Mexican Governor, Juan de Oñate, assigned missionaries to construct a mission and ordered the Pecos people to work as laborers and pay tribute to the Spaniards. In 1680, Pecos joined the Pueblo Revolt against Spanish oppression. In 1692, a Spanish army returned and forced the construction of a walled fortress; the ruins are visible today. Spanish officials arbitrarily appointed Pecos leaders and required permits even to hunt buffalo. From a population of two thousand, Pecos numbers steadily declined from warfare and smallpox. Epidemics in 1738, 1748, and 1776 reduced them to eighty-four survivors. Finally, in 1786, they made peace with the Comanches, their long-term enemies.

Around 1838, twenty surviving Pecos people moved from Pecos Pueblo to join their Towa-speaking cousins at Jemez. Long ago, they had united as one people. The Pecos were not absorbed by the Jemez, but continued to maintain their unique identity. Intermarriage has occurred, but the mothers' Pecos Clan identity is passed on to the children. Pecos spiritual leaders did entrust the Jemez Hunt Society with an important Kachina for the Pecos Bull Dance. The masked bull Porciúncula was built of a wooden frame covered with cloth and painted with corn and melon plants surrounded by a circle filled background. Clowns from the Eagle Watchers' Society dressed up as cowboys and vaqueros who lassoed themselves while supposedly trying to lasso the bull. A classic pueblo depiction of this ceremony was painted in the twentieth century by José Toledo.

Toledo and other Pecos families remain prominent today. I will never forget my visit a decade ago with Pecos people at Jemez. When word spread that a historian for the traditional Hopi was in the village, a meeting was arranged. Pecos elders expressed their heartfelt determination to rebury the bones of ancestors dug up in the 1930s and taken to Yale University. I explained the process of repatriation and recommended patient determination. They gave me a memorable feast and gifts of pottery and baskets.

Bandelier National Monument
(Circa 800 B.C.-1590)

On first visiting Bandelier in Frijoles Canyon, I felt awe and wonder. How was this place created? Who lived there? For whom was it named?

Its history began about 1,000,000 B.C., when a giant volcano rose and twice erupted in the Jemez Mountains fifteen miles to the east. The volcano exploded and collapsed at Valle Grande. When ancient ancestors of Pueblo people moved into the area, they found the pink-grey volcanic rock soft enough to carve out cliff dwellings with stone tools. Some expanded the natural alcoves formed by erosion of canyon walls, bubbly from pockets of volcanic fumes that had risen through the ashes. Imbedded in the basalt canyon walls are volcanic glass and green crystals of olivine. The lava came from a layer called mantle, deep in the Earth.

Tewas and Keresans, among this land's original people, formed many clans, societies, and communities. Cochiti and San Felipe elders trace ancestral roots to Bandelier in Frijoles Canyon. According to tradition, ancestral groups united under the guidance of the Spirit to avoid death and dangers. They promoted good life in harmony with respectful values. Courage to seek new lands came from stories of the twin war gods, *Masewi* and *Oyoyewi*, models for the village chief and war chief, and the Corn Mother, *Iareku*, who embodied the Spirit of the clan mothers. The spirits are said to have come up through a "doorway of the rainbow."

Around 1100, when Chaco was at its zenith, clans began arriving at Bandelier. At Bandelier, they soon began building a four-hundred-room, two- and three-story, circular pueblo called Tyuonyi. Clan symbols were painted and carved inside their homes and kivas and on canyon walls. For example, a detailed rock art design was painted of a being encountering a bear. Within one of the five kivas was a mural of *Avanyu*.

Spiritual organization at Bandelier included eleven societies: Medicine (three divisions: Flint, Giant, Shikami), Koshare Clown Fertility (associated with Flint Medicine Society and Turquoise Kiva), Quirana (associated with Shikami or Shi'kame Medicine Society and Pumpkin Kiva), Snake Society, Fire Society, Ku-sha'li Society, Thunderbird Society (associated with Giant), Cochiti Women's Society, Shru'tzi Society, Kachina Society, and Kwe'rana Society.

Archaeologist-historian Adolph Bandelier became interested in the mysteries of Frijoles Canyon over a century ago. He lived for a while at Cochiti to record oral histories and carefully researched Tyuonyi Pueblo. In 1890, he published a fascinating novel, *The Delightmakers*, in which he developed characters, introduced the drama and re-created a spiritual society. His novel was the first literary attempt to reconstruct a vision of life in an ancient pueblo.

Kuaua "Evergreen" Pueblo, Coronado State Monument (Circa 1300-1680)

After clans began migrating out of the Chaco Canyon and Mesa Verde areas, the twelve-hundred-room Kuaua Pueblo was constructed between Albuquerque and Santa Fe on the east side of the Rio Grande. The Northern Tiwa ancestors of Sandia named this place Kuaua, meaning Evergreen Tree. The Kuaua pueblo, with a perimeter of 350 meters, was the third-largest Great House in New Mexico; Pecos was the largest, and Pueblo Bonito second.

Today, only a small part of the village of Kuaua stands, including a reconstructed kiva. After climbing down the ladder and adjusting to the subdued lighting, one can see an unexpected vision of the Pueblo universe. On the walls, ancient priestly artists painted monumental spiritual figures conducting fertility and rainmaking ceremonies while standing on a rainbow. Colorful parrot feather headdresses on the figures suggest Mesoamerican influence. Life-giving rain and seeds pour from the mouths of eagles and sea gulls in flight. Big fish leap into the sky. *Pahos*, prayer feathers, float from the heavens. These are among the few narrative murals to survive in the Southwest, and have made this pueblo famous.

The murals also show water bubbling magically out of olla pots, perhaps validating migration stories that reveal the secret of survival. When celestial omens instructed that they stop and establish a village in a parched area, a special water jar was buried with prayers—and a new spring appeared as a blessing. If the jar broke, say the ancient legends, strong runners carried a new pot to replace the potent ingredient—salt water from the Pacific Ocean. The Pacific was also the source of shells for heishi bead production.

Kuaua murals depict Pueblo ceremonies, figures, and dress shortly before the arrival of Europeans. Kachina-like dancers wear hand-woven cotton clothing in early Pueblo textile styles. Their white braided sashes feature cotton balls with streaming fringe, symbolizing rain falling from clouds. Contemporary weavers from Hopi, Acoma, San Felipe, and San Juan pueblos still braid these sashes for Kachina dances and wedding ceremonies. The rain-cloud cotton balls are made by wrapping cotton string around braided corn husk or yucca rings.

Dancers wear ceremonial skirts, called kilts. Only one ancient kilt has been preserved intact, so the Kuaua mural depictions are especially precious. Most kilts were black, probably dyed from black sunflower seed, embroidered across the bottom and ornamented with elaborate corner tassels—a style still popular at San Felipe Pueblo.

They also wear long, lacy shirts, similar to crochet-trimmed *Isleta* shirts. On their woven belts are designs created by raising warp strings to the surface, a process called float warp. Similar belts are woven today by Pueblos, Tarahumaras in Mexico, Mayans in Central America, and Incas in Peru. Techniques for weaving twill and plain-weave shoulder blankets also spread along north-south trade routes through the Americas.

The original murals, painted in the fifteenth and sixteenth centuries, were skillfully removed by scientists in the 1930s for preservation in the visitor's center. Then they were reproduced inside the reconstructed kiva.

▶▲ *The sun rises at Pueblo Bonito, Chaco Culture National Historic Park, New Mexico, occupied circa* A.D. *1075 to 1123.*
▶ *Volcanic tuff at Bandelier National Monument, New Mexico, was from a volcanic eruption circa 1,000,000* B.C.

Petroglyph National Monument
(Circa 700-1680)

Over a millennium ago, ancient people began to reflect their spiritual and natural world visions by carving and painting pictures, clan symbols, and pictographic writings on rocks. Spreading across West Mesa, overlooking Albuquerque, New Mexico, is an awe-inspiring example of ancient artistry. Among its most impressive images are "Star People," human and animal-like beings with four-pointed stars for heads. Similar images in Pueblo communities represent *Morning Star Warrior* and *Evening Star Maiden*. Emerging from other stars are the claws of an eagle, messenger between Pueblo people and the spirit world.

Living between the Rio Grande and extinct volcanoes, Pueblo priests from Kachina and other religious societies expressed their ideas of the Upper World, Earth, and the Underworld, filled with spiritual beings. West Mesa was created two hundred thousand years ago by a river of molten lava now frozen black. One by one, five volcanoes erupted, exploding at least six times. A lake of lava fifty miles wide sizzled, steamed, and finally grew cold.

Ancient people found real power in this sacred place and an ideal canvas on which to portray powerful ideas and images. What were they trying to express? Puebloans believe that the Earth and heavens are filled with living spirit. It is never suggested in Pueblo spirituality that the Earth is inanimate, an "it." Instead, Puebloan world views are alive, vibrant, and embody an ongoing process of creation. Lightning, from Father Sky, touches Mother Earth. Encircled crosses express what some call Techua Ikachi, "Together with all nations, we hold this land in peace and harmony."

◄ *Long House, Bandelier National Monument, New Mexico. Bandelier is the ancestral home of Cochiti, San Felipe, and San Ildefonso Clans circa* A.D. *1200 to 1590.* ▲ *Reconstructed kiva and paintings. Coronado State Monument, New Mexico. The area was home to the Kuana Pueblo circa* A.D. *1300 to 1680.*

These crosses also represent migrations of groups of clans into the four directions. When the clans could go no farther, according to ancient instructions, they were to create shrines for the Spirit of the Earth. Petroglyph National Monument preserves the Puebloan testimonies to the sanctity of life and death, as well as the cycles of Sun, Moon, and Stars.

Here are colorful parrots, butterflies, and the Spirit of the Water, *Avanyu*, favored design of the famed contemporary potter, Maria Martinez. *Avanyu*, along with the Kachina spirits, is a powerful force in bringing rains to the Pueblo world. When life is in balance and gentle rains nourish the parched desert, the Southwest is blessed.

From the macrocosm of the universe to the microcosm of personal handprints, this rock art expresses the ancient ancestors' vision of the human experience. Images from the natural world—from rattlesnakes to lizards, eagles to crows, deer to bears, roadrunners to the "Wily Coyote"—play important roles in Pueblo storytelling. The themes are lessons for Pueblo children, about respect for life in harmony with both natural and supernatural worlds.

This site was the crossroads between north and south, east and west. Big game hunters came from across the Great Plains; hunting societies still conduct their ceremonies. Bear ceremonialism came from the north; bears are the most powerful animals in the Southwest, and from their clan great chiefs have come. The great Pacific shell trade came from the west, hence the prevalence of wave images. Even more influential ideas and valuable trade goods came from the south, up the Rio Grande from Mesoamerica.

Kokopelli, the humpbacked flute player, is the most famous spirit to travel north from Mesoamerica. He appears on rocks, especially in the Piedras Marcadas region of Petroglyph National Monument. An ancient fertility figure, some Pueblo storytellers describe *Kokopelli* as a sort of "Don Juan" of the Southwest. It has been said that the seed he distributed included more than just corn, beans, and squash. At Hopi, both male and female *Kokopelli* Kachinas appear at spring fertility ceremonies. I once saw *Kokopelli* maidens chase down teenage boys for an experience intended to inspire respect for the true power of women.

El Morro "The Bluff" National Monument
(Circa 400-1350)

In Zuni tradition, El Morro pueblo, near Mount A'ts'ina in the range now called the Zuni Mountains, was named Heshoda Yalta. Paleolithic and Archaic peoples hunted in this region and built small, pithouse villages down the Zuni River. From this high vantage point, ancient peoples could see anyone entering the upper valley. For almost a millennium, people migrated through, and sometimes settled, this area between Grants and Zuni.

Between 1250 and 1350, three to four thousand people resettled around El Morro. Ancient ancestors of the Zuni, and perhaps others, moved to this higher valley to cope with the drought. Within a generation, seven communities had consolidated in larger, mesa-top pueblos, like apartments built around a central plaza. Rainwater was collected in natural basins and small reservoirs. The presence of two kivas may indicate there was a moiety system. The largest mesa-top pueblo, A'ts'ina, grew to over five hundred rooms before the drought. Occupation ended in the fourteenth century and the clans moved back to Zuni and perhaps other pueblos.

Along the cliffs at Zuni, hundreds of ancient symbols were carved into sandstone walls. Some of the designs may have been created by clans who joined the spiritual Galaxy Society, Newe:kwe, and traveled along the upper Little Colorado River. This branch of the Zuni arrived at El Morro after passing Flute Mountain, renamed Escudilla Peak. They later traveled westward to join their relatives at Zuni Pueblo, completing their long search for the Middle Place in the world.

In the five centuries since, countless travelers have ventured through the valley. Below El Morro stands a natural stone landmark, "Inscription Rock," where explorers carved their names and messages into the soft sandstone. Perhaps the oldest Spanish inscription translates:

> Passed by here the Adelantado Don Juan de Oñate, from the discovery of the Sea of the South, the 16th of April of 1605.

Oñate, under contract to the king of Spain to establish a permanent colony in New Mexico, was proclaimed New Mexico's first governor. Spanish claims of "discovery" confounded original peoples of the Southwest.

Under present laws that protect ancient sites, graffiti and other acts of vandalism are illegal. However, on a large boulder in front of the visitor center, you can carve designs to your heart's content.

Gila Cliff Dwellings
(Circa 7,000 B.C., A.D. 100-1300, post 1350)

Thirty million years ago, two plates of earth crushed together in the southwest New Mexico region of the Gila Cliff Dwellings, creating volcanic cones and eruptions. Over the next ten million years, volcanic ash and lava piled up more than one thousand feet deep. This thick crust then collapsed to form a large caldera. The successive waves of volcanic activity that followed are recorded on the Gila Cliff walls. The final surge from deep within the earth formed a lava dome in the center, still visible today.

The Gila Wilderness basin then became the headwaters of three branches of the Gila River that flow westward to the Sea of Cortez in Baja California. From volcanic gas bubble holes around the upper Gila, feldspar moonstones were formed. Heat rising from beneath the Earth still warms hot springs in the area. Water seeping through porous rock created caves and alcoves. These natural formations were used for shelters as early as 7000 B.C. by Paleolithic peoples. Like time capsules, caves throughout the region have preserved the evidence of ancient habitation, including braided dog-hair sashes, fur and feather robes, yucca sandals and big game hunting equipment.

Around A.D. 100, the Mogollon moved into the region and built pithouses. They were among the first in the Southwest to receive the trade goods and ideas spreading upward from Mesoamerica. Corn, beans, squash, and other vegetable seeds arrived, and by 900 farming supplemented hunting. The warm southern climate was conducive to cotton production, so cotton replaced yucca and other natural fibers for clothing and ceremonial textiles. Their Mimbres neighbors created pottery with elaborate pictorial designs, often of supernatural dimensions. Bats and flying beings, Kachina-like figures, and underwater creatures reflect their views of the Upper, Middle, and Underworlds.

After 1000, Anasazi-style influences came from the north. As architecture advanced, fine stone masonry replaced pithouses. Cliff houses were reinforced. Square stone houses were built in surrounding pueblo sites. The Mogollon cliff dwellings were inhabited through the 1200s.

Tree-ring dating of roof timbers indicates that the main Gila Cliff dwellings were constructed between 1270 and 1290. Ten to fifteen families are believed to have lived there during this period. The residents planted vegetable gardens, hunted, and traded with neighbors, then moved after a few generations.

In the three million acres of surrounding area now preserved as a national forest, two thousand trails exist. Some were traveled in the nineteenth century by Cochise, Mangus Colorado, Victoria, and Geronimo in the Apache quest to remain free.

▲ A "T" shaped doorway at Gila Cliff Dwellings National Monument, New Mexico, circa A.D. 1200 to 1300, signifies the emergence. ▶ Inscription Rock at El Morro National Monument, New Mexico, is an important Zuni site. The area was occupied from about A.D. 400 to 1350.

Ancient Peoples of Colorado

Mesa Verde National Park
(Circa 600-1300)

Over a dozen clan histories tell stories about ancient ancestors who once called Mesa Verde home. Some traditions name specific people and recount their personal experiences while living in these cliff dwellings. Bow, Bear, Antelope, Water, Cloud, Corn, Eagle, Sun, Turkey, Black Badger, Grey Badger, Brown Badger, Butterfly, and Parrot Clans—all lived at Mesa Verde. They carved and painted their clan symbols onto the sandstone mesa walls. Today, most of their descendants live in pueblos throughout Arizona and New Mexico.

The early archaeologists called the original Mesa Verde people Cliff Dwellers, scratched their heads, and reported that these inhabitants simply disappeared sometime during the drought that devasted the area in the late thirteenth century. Contemporary scholars refer to them as Mesa Verde or Northern San Juan Anasazi, because they lived north of the San Juan River that flows nearby. The mesa overlooks two valleys, Montezuma and Mancos.

Mesa Verde's cultural influence spread east through the Mancos, Animas, and Piedra Valleys east of Durango, Colorado, north beyond the San Juan River, west through the Montezuma Valley, and south to Chaco Canyon. People traveled these routes to and from Mesa Verde. The Mesa Verde inhabitants didn't disappear; they migrated to the Rio Grande Valley, Zuni, and Hopi.

Around A.D. 600, shortly after the ancient Tewa ancestors of the San Juan, Santa Clara, San Ildefonso, Nambe, Tesuque, and Pojoaque peoples branched away from the main Tanoan group, permanent settlements formed at Mesa Verde. The traditional place of origin was considered to be less than two hundred miles to the east. The settlements that are today called Basketmaker III featured pithouses where the people made pottery and grew a variety of vegetables, including corn, beans, and squash.

From 800 to 900, as villages spread from Mesa Verde into the Montezuma Valley and east of Blanding on Alkali Ridge, the Northern San Juan people built above-ground, Pueblo-style homes out of clay and sticks. During the 900s, building techniques became more sophisticated, adding

◄ *A kiva is seen through a "T" shaped doorway at Spruce Tree House, Mesa Verde National Park, Colorado. This area was occupied from about A.D. 1200 to 1300.*

sandstone masonry. Kivas expanded into keyhole shapes with the addition of a small room to the south or southeast. By 950, only twenty percent of the people at Mesa Verde lived in the canyon; the rest lived on the mesatop and in outlying areas.

After 1150, two-thirds of the population was concentrated in the southern Mesa Verde canyon, at a time when *Hak'u* Acoma Pueblo and Hopi villages expanded. Approximately 200 miles separated Acoma and Mesa Verde; only 150 miles separated Hopi and Mesa Verde. A determined individual could walk from one pueblo to the other in two weeks. Trained Pueblo runners can cover these distances in three or four days. That there was direct communication is evident.

By 1200, after an elaborate system of roads and trade routes had been established, Mesa Verde pueblos were growing. People at Mesa Verde began constructing cliff dwellings, including Square Tower House, Balcony House, Spruce Tree House, and Long House. A high point in the "Anasazi" world came when master masons completed their finest achievement, Cliff Palace.

The respected Badger clan elder, John Lansa, told me traditional stories of Mesa Verde. Hopi called Mesa Verde *Salapa,* "Place of the Spruce Tree." The Badger, Bear, Butterfly, Eagle, and Parrot Clans helped build these magnificent cliff dwellings. Their last Mesa Verde chief was named *Salavi,* "Spruce."

When the rains stopped falling and the smell of death was in the air, Chief Salavi blamed people's constant quarreling for causing the cataclysm. Corn fields withered and died. Animals migrated away. People faced starvation. Rumors of witchcraft flaired. Chief Salavi concluded that this was not the place of harmony sought in their search for the center of the world.

He called the people together and told them it was time to leave. However, he felt he was too old to travel and instructed them to leave him at Mesa Verde. His last words called for their return in four years. If he was to blame for their calamity, no trace of his existence would remain. But if his heart was good, they would find a sign. Upon their return, according to Badger Clan history, they found water gushing from a spring. Next to it stood a four-year-old spruce tree.

This remarkable story was recorded in symbolic writing at nearby Pictograph Point, with a portrayal of Chief Salavi reincarnated as a tree with spring water flowing to the roots. Today, the spruce, or Douglas fir as it is called today, is respected as a sacred tree, like the Christmas tree or Tree of Life. During spiritual journeys priests select this variety for religious ceremonies of Kachina and other societies.

From 1275 to 1300, the drought tightened its grip. Tanoans moved from upper San Juan and Mesa Verde. They described the drought as a time when "Mother Earth was splitting apart." Drought crept through the Southwest like a demon, choking the life from one and all. With hopes for survival, elders recounted stories of rivers that never ran dry, like the Rio Grande, and springs that never stopped flowing at Hopi, Zuni, and Acoma.

Some ancestors of Zia and Santa Ana, Keresan speakers, began migrating from Mesa Verde and Chaco to the Rio Puerco and Rio Grande. Eastern Keresan-style pottery spread southeast from the Chaco and Mesa Verde regions down the Rio Grande and Rio Puerco Valleys, providing physical evidence today of the oral history traditions that have been handed down.

Today, Mesa Verde stands as America's favorite ancient archaeological site. More than one-half million people visit each year. Mesa Verde's accomplishments inspire profound respect for the Original People of the Southwest and their remarkable creations.

Lowry Pueblo Ruins
(Circa 850-1000, 1060-1200)

In the middle of the eighth century, the Northern San Juan people founded Lowry Pueblo, about thirty miles northwest of Mesa Verde and fifteen miles north of Hovenweep. They dug pithouses, cultivated vegetable gardens, and hunted for meat. The women made fine pottery with attractive designs. A nearby spring provided a fresh water supply that was developed into a small reservoir. In this fertile ground, the seeds of Chacoan and, later, Mesa Verde cultures flourished.

Three centuries later, the little backwater pueblo stood abandoned. Then, around 1085, clans arrived from Chaco Canyon to set up an outlier community. Lowry soon grew into an important center for trade and spirituality. Masons constructed forty-room dwellings that were as much as three stories high. They built eight small kivas around a central Great Kiva forty-five feet in diameter. Population in the area grew to an estimated two thousand people who probably came to Lowry to observe various rituals. Wall murals show designs of kiva steps, symbolic passageways into the Underworld.

During the twelfth century, Mesa Verdeans joined the Chacoan people. The dual presence is evident in two distinct styles of masonry stonework. The two groups lived in harmony. Little evidence of warfare exists. How did these people learn to live together for centuries in relative peace? The answer, Puebloan elders explain, is faith in a higher power whose "Original Divine Instructions" explain how "life is sacred," and "we are all related, endowed with living spirit, part of the Great Spirit."

Soon, more Mesa Verde people lived at Lowry and other pueblos in the Montezuma Valley than had ever lived on the mesa. Thousands of people congregated at Lowry Pueblo, Yellow Jacket Pueblo, and Farview, near Mesa Verde. These three pueblos were connected by a complex of roads both for commerce and for a spirituality that united the people.

Anasazi Heritage Center

The Bureau of Land Management's Anasazi Heritage Center is a federal museum that displays and preserves artifacts and records from research done on public lands in the Four Corners area. It is located at the sites of Dominguez and Escalante Pueblos. Don't miss the Discovery Room, featuring microscopes, computers, and hands-on exhibits. Grind the blue corn on metates, and imagine young Romeos courting fair maidens who had been set to this task. Mamas investigated what their daughters were up to if the sound of grinding stopped. Explore a replica of a late ninth-century pithouse. Here is the model that evolved into ritual kivas. The temporary gallery regularly rotates a variety of exhibits focusing on modern Native American culture.

The Anasazi Heritage Center staff currently manages two million artifacts, samples, and documents. Most of the materials represent Northern San Juan Anasazi culture and were recovered during the Dolores Archaeological Program, the largest single archaeological project in the history of the United States. Researchers identified and mapped about sixteen hundred Anasazi sites—including hunting camps, shrines, granaries, households, and villages—along the Dolores River in the project area. They excavated or tested 120 sites in order to prevent destruction of their information value by the reservoir. Many items are on display in the museum; the rest are available for study and research.

Dominguez and Escalante Pueblos
(Circa 1123-1225 and 1129-1225)

For about a century, Northern San Juan people lived in these two pueblos near the Anasazi Heritage Center. In

▲ A Mancos black-and-white bowl created in the Pueblo III period is displayed at the Edge of the Cedars State Park, Utah.
▶ Mesa Verde towers above the valley floor at Mesa Verde National Park, Colorado. This area was occupied by a variety of clans from about A.D. 600 to 1300.

August 1776, two Catholic friars rested here on a journey from Santa Fe to California. During the twentieth century, the pueblos were named for the two friars—Dominguez and Escalante. At this site, and at many of the other ancient sites in the Southwest, the original names of the pueblos are unknown.

Dominguez Pueblo became the final resting place for a woman who died when she was thirty-five. She wore over sixty-nine hundred precious beads with turquoise mosaics and frog pendants. The bejeweled woman's four-room final resting place and kiva were built in 1123 of "Northern Anasazi" style. Although her wealth was rare, her identity remains a mystery, shrouded in the mists of time.

The frog, to which the woman's jewelry paid tribute, is important in Pueblo society because its song calls the rain. The Hopi Frog Clan, part of the *Patki* Water/Cloud group, recount their Southern Anasazi origins at Homol'ovi and Montezuma's Castle. In the late 1000s or early 1100s, a dramatic change occured in spirituality, including a change in death rituals. New symbols of toads, frogs, and raptorial birds appeared. Gourd rasps in Hopi ceremonies emulate the sounds of frogs croaking. Frogs often appear next to images of the Mesoamerican Water god *Tlaloc*. This important deity is associated with the jaguar, the serpent, and the feathered serpent.

In the late A.D. 1000s, construction began on Escalante Pueblo on a hill overlooking Dominguez Pueblo. After a decade, the builders moved on, and the village was reinhabited by two groups of Northern San Juan people. They expanded the block of rooms. The two kivas may indicate a moiety system of Tanoan or Keresan origin. Shortly after 1200, at a time when Chaco began to fade and Mesa Verde was experiencing a cultural flowering, the people abandoned their pueblo.

Ute Mountain Tribal Park
(Circa 600-1250)

Thousands of ancient sites exist south of Mesa Verde, within a 125-thousand-acre preserve under the jurisdiction of the Ute Mountain Tribe. Today, Ute Indian guides lead small groups through the park, which features Eagle Nest, Tree House, Lion House, Morris V, and Two Story Cliff Dwelling.

In the deep canyons are Mesa Verde–style cliff dwellings. Pueblos rise along river valleys filled with colorful rock art. Around 1200, the people at Eagle Nest began to construct cliff dwellings similar to Spruce Tree House at Mesa Verde. Their vegetable gardens remained on top of the mesa.

◄ ▲ *Square Tower Ruin, Mesa Verde National Park, Colorado. This area was occupied from about* A.D. *1200 to 1300.* ◄ *Pithouse at Step House Ruin, Mesa Verde National Park, Colorado, was occupied from about* A.D. *600 to 900.*

Utes speak a Uto-Aztecan language that is related to the Paiute, Shoshone, Comanche, and Hopi. They adopted Plains influences in dress and gained fame as great buffalo hunters and horsemen. Ute war shirts are often yellow and green with a long fringe and bold beadwork. Their medicine people are both men and women. They participate in vision quests and the Sun Dance like the Comanche, Kiowa, and Sioux. In the Ute world view, life is infused with spiritual power.

The Ute Mountain Tribe preserves over a half million acres of land. The Ute people are to be commended for their great effort to build a better future for themselves and for their children.

Chimney Rock Archaeological Area
(Circa 925-1125)

The pueblo at Chimney Rock is like the Peruvian mountain top sanctuary of Machu Picchu in the Andes. Built by master Chaco engineers, it stands at seventy-five hundred feet in elevation. When was it built, and why?

One theory is that a group of Chaco priests arrived around 1075. That was the year when, in October, the moon appeared to freeze in place after rising between twin pinnacles atop Chimney Rock. Astronomers attribute this phenomenon to a lunar cycle that repeats every 18.6 years. In 1076, according to tree ring dating, a mammoth construction effort began to build of a Chaco-style pueblo. On March 7 of that year, a total solar eclipse darkened the sky, an event predictable by astronomers. If Chaco priests calculated those lunar and solar cycles, as did Toltec astronomers, the rural people around Chimney Rock witnessed the truth of the priests' predicitons.

The traditional Taos elders view Chimney Rock with respect. This holy shrine is devoted to two cultural heroes, the Pueblo Twin War Gods. Tradition holds that their guidance after the emergence into the Fourth World is the ideal of strong leadership. The Twin War Gods protected the people and served as role models for chiefs, war chiefs and Bow Priests.

Some say the twins are the offspring of the Sun and Yellow Woman, a mortal from the north, and grandchildren of Spider Woman, an Earth goddess. They respond to the prayers of rainmakers and evoke fertility. Their powers aid in the hunt. Stories of the twins' childhood describe their mischievous side and contain lessons drawn from brotherly rivalries. The elder brother often takes the lead. When he fails, the younger brother eagerly tries to succeed. Sometimes their adventures put them in life-threatening danger, but at the last moment Spider Grandmother comes to their rescue. Her spirit represents the universal wisdom of grandmothers. The twins listen, but soon are off on another daring adventure. Mamma always sets the record straight in the end. She has faith that her children are blessed with potential greatness.

Epilogue

At a meeting between United Nations Assistant Secretary General Robert Muller and Hopi religious leaders, an elder gave the Indian version of a story we were all taught in school:

I found that when Columbus, somebody by the name of Columbus, came to this land, he claimed to discover this land. But we were the ones, our ancestors, who discovered him, fooling around, lost in the ocean. And maybe he's full of rum.

He was sure he had landed in India. So he kept calling us Indians . . . We're not Indians. We're not from that country . . . We live in these villages that people call Pueblo. Our name means peace, kind, gentle and truthfulness.

Introducing traditional knowledge and religious beliefs, the Bluebird chief took a global perspective:

. . . individual human beings [of] different races have certain basic views that guide them . . . to carry on that life. Looking into the future, how [will] they arrive there at a good life ahead. There is always a desire on the part of every human being to try and use that power that was given him by a higher being . . . that is the basic thing in every individual. So we cannot say that we don't have any power. Each one has power.

◄ *Aligned doorways present an interesting design at West Ruin in Aztec Ruins National Monument, New Mexico. The area was occupied from about A.D. 1106 to 1300.* ▲ *A Sundog watches over Hopi Reservation, Third Mesa, Arizona. Celestial phenomenon often are viewed as omens.*

Dr. Muller, the grand old philosopher of the United Nations, responded:

What you have just said at the end about the power of the individual person, that each individual person has a power that has been given to him by the Supreme Being, I would like you to say what you know about the power of the individual, as he gets it from the Supreme Being. A statement on this subject would be a revelation. It would be a benefit to millions of people on this planet.

In 1984, when we sat clustered in the Kachina House for four days and nights to listen as the high spiritual leaders recited prophecies, the Bluebird Chief advised:

. . . we must remember that in our work in the future to see if we can use that power. We believe something. We shall pray and meditate and think over on the principle that we [are] following. Maybe out of which we will receive the power to do something right.

Each person, he said, may find power through meditation and prayer—inside themselves, around themselves, and around others. A group of people also are capable of uniting their power:

Even though it looks like they don't have power . . . that power is great . . . They are underneath that structure that we are following, those spiritual values that still need to be brought out. Sooner or later maybe, you people will really start searching and . . . you may find out through your ways your power is still great . . . Let us remember also that we . . . will put our thoughts together and assure that we can bring about a peaceful solution . . . without destroying one another with all the power.

Pueblo chiefs in the Rio Grande carry ceremonial canes that symbolize the power of their sovereignty. Those canes were presented in 1620 by King Charles IV of Spain and in 1854 by President Abraham Lincoln to recognize the sovereign power of the Pueblos. Former Santa Clara Governor Walter Dasheno explained:

We honor the transfer of the canes . . . We also pray for a good year for everyone on this earth, so they will be able to interact with the good things in life . . . At this time, with the gaming issues, land and water rights and guarantee of their native beliefs, people have got to really understand the significance of those canes. Today, it's a message of what needs to be recognized in those rights, and understood that these rights were upheld by the President and Congress and by a king and the monarchy of Spain when they gave us those canes of authority.

When the canes of authority are passed on to the next chief or governor, Buffalo and Deer dances are performed. Everyone is invited to attend these ceremonies the first weekend each January.

You are also invited to visit the sites described in these chapters. Walk softly, act respectfully, recognize history came before Columbus and remember you have power—the power to preserve peace on Earth.

Clans and Sites

This book, first in a series on the history and cultures of the Ancient Southwest, reflects fifteen years of intensive research dedicated to gaining a better understanding of our regional heritage.

The stories it contains are authentic, gleaned from oral histories of more than two hundred clans. Handed down from generation to generation and related with care by respected elders, these stories contain important lessons for all of us from a long and valued human experience.

Information gleaned from the epic migration sagas, blended with archaeological evidence and archival research, gives us this new look at ancient dwelling sites, and the lives of the people who called them home. This book is based on tracing clans back to their original dwelling places. Here, in summary, are the cultures and clans that are connected with each site described in previous chapters.

ARIZONA

Grand Canyon National Park
Archaic-P V:
Circa 8000 B.C.- present
Hakatayan, Hisatsinom, Hopi, Havasupai, Walapai.
Clans: Bear, Snake, Mountain Lion, Dove, Cholla Cactus, Opuntia Cactus, Nabovu, Horn, Deer, Antelope, Tcaizra, Badger, Ant

Casa Grande "Grand House" Ruins National Monument
Pueblo IV:
Circa 1350-1450
Hohokam, Hopi, Pima, Papago

Canyon de Chelly "Rocky Canyon" National Monument
Basketmaker II-Pueblo III:
Circa 350-1300
Hopi.
Clans: Badger, Butterfly, Tansy Mustard
Circa 1700-present
Diné

Petrified Forest National Park
Basketmaker II-Pueblo V:
Circa 6000 B.C.-20th century
Basketmakers, Mogollon, Ancesral Puebloan, Hakataya, Sinagua, Hopi, Zuni

Homol'ovi Ruins State Park
Pueblo III-IV:
Circa 1250-1600
Hopi, Zuni.
Clans: Squash, Flute, Blue-Green Flute, Drab Flute, Mountain Sheep, Water, Cloud, Young Corn, Rabbitbrush, Frog, Tadpole, Snow, Sand/Earth, Lizard, Rabbit, Tobacco, Sun Forehead, Sun, Hawk, Badger, Kachina Badger, Porcupine, Turkey Buzzard, Butterfly, Kachina, Parrot, Yellow Bird, Yellow Finch, Spruce, Cottonwood, Crow

Montezuma Castle National Monument
Basketmaker III-Pueblo IV:
Circa 600-1400
Hohokam, Hakataya, Sinagua, Hopi.
Clans: Bear Strap, Water, Cloud, Young Corn, Frog, Tadpole, Snow, Sun Forehead

Tuzigoot "Crooked Water" National Monument
Pueblo II-IV:
Circa 900-1450
Hohokam, Sinagua, Hopi, Zuni

Walnut Canyon National Monument
Pueblo III:
Circa 1050-1275
Sinagua, Hopi, Zuni

Wupatki "Tall House" National Monument & Sunset Crater
Paleolithic, Archaic, Basketmaker I-Pueblo III:
Circa 9000-6000 B.C., 5000-2000 B.C., 500-675, 675-1064, 1075-1225
Clovis, Agate Basin, Archaic, Sinagua, Hakataya, Kayenta, Hisatsinom, Winslow, Prescott, Cohonina [Hopi for Grand Canyon peoples], Mogollon, Salt-Gila River Hohokam, Hopi Bear Clan

Navajo National Monument:
Betatakin "Ledge House" and Keet Seel "Broken Pottery"
Pueblo II-Pueblo III:
Circa 950-1300
Kayenta, Hopi.
Clans: Bear, Snake, Mountain Lion, Dove, Cholla Cactus, Opuntia Cactus, Nabovu, Horn, Deer, Antelope, Tcaizra, Badger, Ant

UTAH

Hovenweep "Deserted Canyon" National Monument
Basketmaker III-Pueblo III:
Circa 500-1290
San Juan, Mesa Verde, Ute, Hopi

Edge of the Cedars State Park
Pueblo I-Pueblo III:
Circa 800-950, 1025-1125, 1200-1300
Northern San Juan, Mesa Verde

Mule Canyon, Cedar Mesa Area
Pueblo I-Pueblo III:
Circa 750-1300
Kayenta and Mesa Verde

Natural Bridges National Monument
Basketmaker II-Pueblo III:
Circa 1-1300
Kayenta, Mesa Verde, Fremont, Hopi, Tewa

Grand Gulch Primitive Area
Basketmaker II-Pueblo III:
Circa 200-1300
Basketmakers, San Juan

Anasazi Indian Village State Park or Coombs Site
Pueblo II-III:
Circa 1075-1275
Kayenta

Newspaper Rock and Canyonlands National Park
Archaic-Pueblo III:
Circa 7000 B.C.-A.D. 1300
Archaic, Basketmakers, Fremont, San Juan, Ute

Fremont Indian State Park
Pueblo I-Pueblo III:
Circa 875-1250
Sevier Fremont, Kayenta, Hopi, Uto-Aztecan, Numic, Paiute, Ute, Shoshone, Athabaskan, Navajo, Apache

Three Kiva Pueblo
Pueblo II-III:
Circa 900-1300
San Juan, Kayenta, Mesa Verde, Hopi, Ute

NEW MEXICO

Chaco Canyon National Historical Park
Archaic-Pueblo III:
Circa 7,000 B.C.-A.D. 1300
Eastern Hisatsinom, Keresans, Hopi, Zuni, Tanoans, Taos.
Clans: Bear, Sun, Badger, Deer, Antelope, Water, Cloud, Corn, Eagle

Aztec Ruins National Monument
Pueblo III:
Circa 1100-1200 and 1125-1300
Eastern San Juan River, Hisatsinom, Chaco and later
Mesa Verde peoples, Keresans, Hanu Santa Ana.
Clans: Corn, Sun, Eagle, Dove, Turkey, Fire, Water, Coyote, Mouse, Badger, and Yashcha

Pecos National Historical Park
Pueblo II-IV:
Circa 850-1838
Ancestral Puebloan, Pecos people now live at Jemez Pueblo.
Clans: Bear, Fire, Sun, Cloud, Corn, Turquoise, Coyote, Badger, Earth or Sand, Deer, Crow, Eagle, Calabash Squash, Piñon, Ant, Mountain Lion, Buffalo, Oak, Elk, Antelope, Snake, Parrot, Turkey

Bandelier National Monument
Basketmaker I-Pueblo IV:
Circa 800 B.C.-1590
Ancestral Puebloan, Cochiti, San Felipe, San Ildefonso.
Clans: Bear, Mountain Lion, Squash, Deer, Antelope, Water, Cloud, Corn, Fire, Coyote, Eagle, Sun, Turkey, Cottonwood, Red Shell, Turquoise, Oak, Ivy, Sage, Dance Kilt, Shipewe, Elk

Kuaua "Evergreen" Pueblo, Coronado State Monument
Pueblo IV:
Circa 1300-1680?
Ancestral Puebloan, Mogollon, Tigua, Santa Ana, Sandia.
Clans: Corn, Sun, Eagle, Dove, Turkey, Fire, Water, Coyote, Mouse, Badger, and Yashcha All Kinds of Beads

Petroglyph National Monument
Pueblo I-IV:
Circa 700-1680?

El Morro "The Bluff" National Monument
Basketmaker III-Pueblo IV:
Circa 400-1350
Mogollon, Ancestral Puebloan, Zuni

Gila Cliff Dwellings
Basketmaker II-Pueblo III:
Circa 7,000 B.C., A.D. 100-1300, post 1350
Paleolithic, Mogollon, Apache

COLORADO

Mesa Verde National Park
Basketmaker III-Pueblo III:
Circa 600-1300
Mesa Verdean, Northern San Juan, Cliff Dwellers, Basketmakers, Acoma, Hopi, Cochiti, Laguna, San Felipe, Santa Ana, Santo Domingo, Zia, Taos, Sandia, Isleta, San Juan, Santa Clara, San Ildefonso, Nambe, Tesuque, Jemez, Pecos and Zuni.

Lowry Pueblo Ruins
Pueblo I-Pueblo III:
Circa 850-1000, 1060-1200
Northern San Juan, Chacoan, Mesa Verdean

Dominguez and Escalante Pueblos
Pueblo II-Pueblo III:
Circa 1123-1225 and 1129-1225
Chacoan, Mesa Verdean, Hopi

Ute Mountain Tribal Park
Basketmaker III-Pueblo IV:
Circa 600-1250
Mesa Verdean, Ute

Chimney Rock Archaeological Area
Pueblo I-Pueblo II:
Circa 925-1125
Chacoan, Tiwa, Taos

Index

A'alt Two Horn Society 53
Acoma 13, 16, 29, 30, 33, 40, 62, 69-70
Agate House 43
Ahayuda 43
Ala Horn Clan 33, 34
Alkali Ridge 69
Alta Vista 30
American Museum of Natural History 53
Anasazi Heritage Center 70
Anasazi Indian Village SP 53
Ancient Indian Ruin **51**
Animas Valley 69
Antelope Clan/House/Mesa 34, 35, 43, 54, 69
Anwuci Clan 34
Apache 13, 39, 54
Aquarious Plateau 53
Archaic Period 24, 39, 65
Ard, Raymond 20
Arroyo Hondo 35
Asa Wild Mustard Clan 43
Athabascan 25, 34, 54
Atlatl 49, 57
Atoko Crane Clan 34
A'ts'ina 66
Austin, Virginia 7
Avanyu 30, 36, 40, 61, 62, 65
Awatovi 34, 36, 43, 53
Aztec people/Ruins 5, 33, 36, 40, 58, **59, 74**
Badger Clan 16, 35-36, 44-45, 69
Bahnimptewa, Jacob 16
Balcony House 69
Bandelier, Adolph 62
Bandelier NM 16, 35, **60**, 61-62, **63, 64**
Basketmaker I, II, III Periods 25-26, 53, 69
Bat Cave 25, 45
Bear Clan 14, 24, 26, 29, 35, 39, 45, 53, 54, 69
Beautiful House 46
Belt (human hair) **36**
Benedict, Dr. Ruth 13
Berenholtz, James 7
Besh-ba-gowah Pueblo **40**
Betatakin 16, 33, 46, 54
Big Fire Society 57
Bluebird Clan 14, 24, 26, 29, 75
Bluefish Caves 23
Blue Flute 54
Boas, Franz 13
Bow Clan 24, 39, 57, 69
Bowl (Mancos B&W) **70**
Bronfman, Jeffrey 7
Broome, Michael 7
Buffalo dancers 40
Butterfly Clan 16, 35, 69
Cahokia 34
Canyon de Chelly 2, 16, 26, 40, 43, **46**
Canyon del Muerto 40
Canyonlands NP **11, 22**, 53
Casa Grande 30, 39-40
Casa Rinconada **58**
Castaño de Sosa, Gaspar 61
Cave of the Fleas 23
Cedar Mesa **51**
Cerillos 34
Cenozoic Era 20
Chaco Canyon 16, 24-26, 30, **32**, 33-35, 37, 43, 49, 53, **56**, 57, **58**, 62, **63**, 69, 70, 70
Charles IV (of Spain) 75
Chaves Pass 36, 44
Chetro Ketl 34, 57
Chimik'yana'kya deya 39
Chimney Rock Archaeological Area 73
Cinq-Mars, Jacques 23
Cliff Palace 69
Cloud Clan 35, 40, 69, 73
Clovis 24, 45
Cochise Desert 24

Cochiti 13, 16, 35, 62
Cohonina 39
Comanches 61
Copan 25
Corn Clan/Dance/ Petroglyph **28**, 33, 35, 69
Coronado SM **65**
Crane Clan 53
Craner, Bob 7
Cressman, L. S. 23
Crow Clan 34
Cunkle, James 7
Cutthroat Ruins **Back Cover**
Dasheno, Walter 75
Death Valley 19
Deer Clan 14, 53
Delores Archaeological Program 70
Desert Archaic 54
Deserted Canyon 49
Diné Navajo 7, 13, 31, 34, 36, 39, 43, 46, 54
Dominguez Ruins 70, 73
Eagle Clan/Nest/Watchers 35-36, 61, 69, 73
Edge of the Cedars SP **7, 9, 13, 19, 29, 36, 39, 49, 57, 69, 70, 75, 76, 78**
El Morro NM 65, **67**
Escalante Ruins 70, 73
Espejo, Antonio de 61
Farview 53
Fein, Bob 7
Fewkes, Walter Jessie 26, 43, 46
Fifth World 57
First Mesa 16, 43
First World 14
Fish Canyon 50
Flattop site 43
Flute Clan 34, 46, 54
Freire-Marreco, B. 13
Fourth World 15, 34, 39-40, 57
Fremont Indian SP 54
Frijoles Canyon 61-62
Frog Clan 40, 73
Furada, Pedra 23
Galaxy Society 66
Galindo, Mazatl 7
Galisteo 35
Gallina 35
Giant Ogre 35, 44
Gila people/Cliff Dwellings 20, 25, 30, 34, **66**
Gogyeng Sowahti 14, 15
Governador area 25, 61
Grand Canyon 13, 19, 24-25, 39 **38**, 39
Grand Gulch Primitive Area 53
Great Kiva 34, **58, 59**, 70, 73
Grey Badger Clan 69
Grey Flute Clan 54
Guidon, Niede 23
Halona 15
Hanau 26
Hanu 35-36
Handprints **26, 50**
Hanlibinkya 43
Harrington, John Peabody 13
Harwood, Frances 7
Havasupai 13, 39
Heard Museum 7
Hermaquaftewa, Andrew 29
Hisatsinom 25
Hognyam Bear Clan 39
Hohokam 25-26, 30, 33-36, 40, 44-46, 53, 73
Hokan 25, 39
Holly Castle **55**
Homol'ovi people/II **20**, 34-36, 43-44, 46, 73
Hopi 9-10, 13, 15-16, 24-26, 29-30, 36, 39-40, 43, 44, 45, 46, 57-58, 62, 69-70, 73, 75
Hopiland 24, 26, 39
Horn Clan 33-34, 46, 53, 54
Horseshoe Canyon Maze/Ruins **26**, 54
Hovenweep NM **26**, 35, **48**, 49, **50**, 54, **55**, **Back Cover**

Hughes, Ken 7
Huwi Dove Clan 33
Iareku 62
Inscription Rock 66, **67**
Institute of American Indian Arts 7
Isleta people 13, 30, 36, 62
Ivy Creek pottery 54
Iyatiko 16
Jacona 33
Jalisco 30
Jemez 13, 16, 25, 35-36, 45, 61
Jettipehika 36
Johanson, Donald C. 20
Kachina 16, 34-36, 43, 44, 50, 53, 57, 62, 65
Kaibab Plateau 39
Kakora 61
Katchongva, Dan 14
Katsina/Katsinyam 16
Kayenta 25, 34, 43, 44, 45, 53, 54
Keet Seel (or Kiet Siel) 16, 33, **42**, 45, 46, 54
Kele Clan 34
Kemper, Ellen 7
Keresan 16, 25-26, 30, 33, 35, 40, 58, 61-62, 70
Kikmongwi 29, 39
Kimmey, John 7
Kiowa-Tanoan 30
Kisiu-va 36
Kiva **1**, 65, **68**, 69
Kokop Fire Clan 35
Kokopelli **8**, 30, 65
Koluwala:wa 43
Kostenki 23
Kuaua Pueblo 62
Kunchalpi 36
Kuskurza 14
Kwan One Horn Society 53
Kwiiste Kene'wa 36
Kwinapa 36
Kyashngyam 16
Ladder (kiva) **80**
Laguna 13, 16, 40
Lansa, John 45, 69
Lascaux Cave 23
Leaky, Dr. Mary D. 20
Lehner Kill Site 24
Lenya Clan 34
Lincoln, Abraham 75
Lightning Man 34, 57
Lion House 73
Llano Estaciado 24
Lomaki Ruin **46**
Long House **64**, 69
Lowry Pueblo 49, 53, 70
Maasaw 14-16, 29, 35, 44
MacNeish, Richard 23
Mancos 69, **70**
Mano **5, 29**
Mesa Verde NP 16, 23-26, 30, 33, 35, 43, 49, 53, 54, 58, 62, **68**, 69, 70, **71, 72**, 73
Masewi 16, 62
Matate **29**
Meteor Crater 23
Middle Place 50, 58, 66
Middle World 40
Moche 25
Mogollon 10, 18, 24-26, 30, 34, 36, 43, 66
Mongkohu 39
Monkey Clan 14
Monongye, David 9
Monte Alban 25
Montezuma Castle/Valley 16, 20, 35, **41**, 44, 49, 53, 69, 73
Moreno, Fidel 7
Mudhead 35, 44
Mug, black-on-white **6**
Mui-aingwa 19
Mule Canyon 50
Muller, Robert 75
Mummy Cave 40-41

Museum of the American Indian 53
Museum of Indian Arts & Cultures 7
Nachwach Symbols **6**
Nahuatl-Aztec 40
Nakbe 25
Nalakihu 46
Nambe 13, 16, 26, 33, 36, 57, 69
National Museum of American Indian Arts 7
National Museum of American Indian 7, 53
Natural Bridges NM 50, 53
Newspaper Rock 53
Niman Home Dance 34
Nuvatikyao 45
Oga'akeneh 16
Ojo Caliente 33
Old Crow Basin 23
Old Mishonognovi 34
Old Oraibi 45
Olmec 25, 57
Oñate, Juan de 61, 66
Oraibi 36, 45
Orogrand Cave 23
Ortiz, Alfonso 25
Otowi 35
Oweweham'baiyo 33
Oyoyewi 16, 62
Paak'u Pueblo 35, 70
Paayu 43
Paiute 13, 25, 53, 54
Pajarito Plateau 35, 35
Pakatcomo 36
Palatki Ruin, Red Cliffs **18**
Palatkwabi 36, 44
Paleolithic Period 23-24
Paleozoic Period 19
Palulukon 36, 40
Papago 13, 25, 39-40
Parrot Clan 16, 35, 69
Parsons, Elsie Clews 13, 33
Patki Water Clan 40, 73
Patun Clan 26, 33
Payupki 35
Pecos **1**, 13, 25, 35-36 58, 61, 62
Pe-Kush 61
Pela, Earl 29
Penasco Blanca 33
Petrified Forest NP **30**, 43
Petroglyph NM 65
Phoenix Basin 34
Picuris 13, 30, 36
Pigeon Clan 34
Piki 43
Pima 13, 25, 30, 40
Pindi Pueblo 35
Pingkuwaiye 33
Pithouse **72**
Pleistocene Period 20, 23
Pojoaque 13, 16, 26, 33, 35-36, 57, 69
Posijumu 33
Posipopi 33
Post Pleistocene/Archaic Period 24-25
Pot Creek Pueblo 35
Potsuwi 33, 35
Pottery Mound 35-36
Porciúncula 61
Powamu 34, 53, 57
Powell, John Wesley 39
Precambrian Era 19
Prince, Todd 7
Pueblo Bonito **32**, 33-34, 53, **56**, 57, 62, **63**
Pueblo del Arroyo 37
Pueblo I, II, III, IV Periods 29-30, 34-35
Pueblo Revolt 26, 61
Puerco Ruin 43
Quamahongnewa, Radford 7
Quetzalcoatl 40, 61
Raven Site **27**, 44
Reunion Symbols **6**

Rio Grande 57-58, 69-70, 75
Rio Puerco 58, 70
Road Canyon 50
Salapa 69
Salavi 35, 69
Salt River 25, 35
Sand Clan 44
Sandia people/place/Cave 13, 24, 30, 35-36
Sandals (yucca) **22**
Sandstone tableta **27**
San Felipe 13, 16, 35, 62
San Francisco Peaks **20**
San Juan 13, 16, 25-26, 33, 35-36, 49, 57, 62
San Ildefonso 13, 16, 26, 33, 35-36, 57, 69
Santa Ana 58, 70
Santa Clara 13, 16, 26, 33, 36, 57, 69, 75
Santo Domingo 13, 16, 43
Schaafsma, Polly 25
Second Mesa 35-36, 44
Second World 14
Sevier Fremont villages 54
Sevier Gray pottery 54
Shabik'eshchee Village 26, 57
Shaman's Gallery 25, 39
Shonkyuget 16
Shoshone 13, 54
Shungopavi 26, 36, 45
Sibabi 36
Sikyatki Polychrome 35
Sinagua 13, 34-36, 45
Sio Shalako 35, 44
Sipapu 39, 50
Siu-va 36, 45
Sliding Rock 43
Snake Clan 26, 33-35, 46, 53, 54
Snaketown 25, 30, 35
Sotukeu-nangwi 14
Soyoko Ogre 35
Spider Clan/Woman 24, 73
Spruce Tree House **68**, 69, 73
Square Tower House 69, **72**
Squash Clan 26, 33, 61
Star People 65
Step House Ruin **72**
Stoneman Lake 44
Strap Clan 26
Sun god/Clan 14, 44, 35, 58, 69, 73
Sundog, Hopi Reservation **75**
Sun Forehead Clan 36, 44
Sunset Crater NM **12**, 13, 34, 44
Supai 39
Sword Swallower Society 57
Tadpole Clan 40
Taiowa 14
Tanoan 25, 26, 30, 36, 57, 58, 61, 69
Taos 13, 16, 30, 35-36, 58, 73
Tawa 35, 44
Tcua Snake Clan 26, 33, 34
Tcua-wimpkias Snake 34
Tcub-wimpkias Antelope 34
Teotihuacán 25
Tepehuan 30
Tertiary Period 20
Tesuque 13, 16, 26, 33, 36, 54, 57, 69
Tewa 15-16, 25-26, 30-31, 33, 35-36, 50, 57, 62, 69
Third World 15, 40
Three Kiva Pueblo 49, 54
Tiahuanaco 26
Tikal 25, 30
Tiwa 30, 35-36, 62
Tlaloc 35, 40. 73
Tobacco Clan 44
Tohono O'odham 36, 40
Toho Puma Clan 33
Tokonabi 26, 33-34, 46, 54
Tokpa 14
Tokpela 14
Toledo 61

Toltec 25, 34
Tonto NM **16, 17**
Towa 15, 25, 35, 61
Treaty of Guadalupe Hidalgo 9
Tree House 73
Triassic Age 19, 43
Tsakwaina 35
Tsiiyame 36
Tsankawi 33, 35
Tsegi Canyon **31**, 43, **46**
T-shaped doorway **66**
Tsugnyam Snake people 39
Tubec Sorrow-making Clan 34
Tularosa Cave 25, 30
Turkey Clan 35, 69
Turquoise people 61
Tusayan 39-40
Tuwanacabi 36, 44
Tuwaqachi 15, 39
Tuzigoot NM 20, 35, 44
Twin War Gods 14, 16, 62, 73
Twiiste Puu Tamaya 36
Two Story Cliff Dwelling 73
Tyuonyi Pueblo 62
Ucu Cactus Clan 33
Una Vida 33
U. of Arizona/Colorado/New Mexico/Utah 7
Underworld 14, 40, 65
Unnamed Ruin **Front Cover, 52, 54**
Unshagi 61
Upper World 65
Utcevaca 36
Ute Mountain Tribal Park 7, 13, 25, 43, 54, 73
Uto-Aztec 25, 33, 39-40, 54, 58, 73
Uwipinge 33
Valle Grande 61
Vásquez de Coronado, Francisco 61
Ventana Cave 24
Verde Valley 20, 44
Wajima 14
Wakwijo 50
Walapai 13
Walnut Canyon NM 44
Walpi 34, 36, 43, 44
Warrior Kachina Woman Clan 40
Washo 53
Water Clan/god/Spider 15, 35-36, 40, 44, 69, 73
Watu 50
Wavinatita 61
West Ruin **74**
Wetherill, Richard 53
Wheelright Museum 7
White Dog Cave 25
White House Ruin **2**, 16, 43
White Mountain **27, 29**, 43
Wild Mustard Clan 16, 43
Wily Coyote 65
Wind Spirit 45
Wukoko Big House 46
Wupatki NM **10**, 45, **46**
Yaponcha 45
Yavapai 13
Yellow Jacket Pueblo 53, 70
Yellow Woman 73
Young Corn Clan 40
Yunu Opuntia Cactus Clan 33
Zacateca 30
Zia 13, 16, 58, 61, 70
Zuni 13, 15-16, 24-26, 29-30, 33, 36, 39, 43-44, 57-58, 65-66, 69-70

► ► *A ladder provides entry to a reconstructed kiva at Kuana Pueblo, Coronado State Monument, New Mexico.* Back Cover Photograph: *Cutthroat Ruins, Hovenweep National Monument, Utah.*